Portrait of -
MACCLESFIELD

DOUG PICKFORD

Sigma Leisure - Wilmslow

First published in 1988 by
Sigma Leisure, an imprint of **Sigma Press** 1 South Oak Lane, Wilmslow, SK9 6AR
Reprinted with slight revisions, 1993.

British Library Cataloguing in Publication Data

Pickford, D
      Portrait of Macclesfield
      1. Cheshire. Nacclesfield. History
      I. Title
      942.7'16

ISBN: 1-85058-113-4

Cover design and layout: Colin Ellis

Cover photograph: Macclesfield market place, *ca.* 1903, showing the old Angel Hotel (demolished in the early sixties), and the former Parr's Bank, now the National Westminster Bank buildings.

Printed and bound by: Manchester Free Press

Acknowledgments: Hilary Pickford; Kate, Robin and Charles Pickford; Mrs Mary Bullock; Mrs F.R.Gee; Mr King of Bollington; Ursula Arden; Mrs M.Duffield; Mr and Mrs V. Faulkner and all the kind people who have loaned photographs to me over the years and anyone who has helped in any way.

Contents

Chester Road, 1890, or possibly before. Just out of the picture is the Regency Mill. What looks like a huge hole in the foreground is, in fact, a tear in the photograph!

The district near Chester Road extending from St Alban's R.C. Church to Broken Cross was once called Gallows Field and tradition says executions took place there.

1 Early History

Macclesfield and its surrounding villages abound in history and legend - a far cry indeed from their present status as a busy town and peaceful, picturesque hamlets. But first things first - how did Macclesfield begin? Well, legend has it that Macclesfield was once called Hameston,"the settlement on the rock."

Whilst we may never know the truth of this, there is no doubt that the earliest of settlers converged on the flat land where the Parish Church and Town Hall now stand. They would have been afforded natural protection and good farming, with water from the river in the valley.

In the 10th century, the Saxon villages were grouped into areas called Hundreds and Macclesfield (or Hameston) was the centre of trade, justice and government of the Hameston Hundred. Indeed, a court for the Forest of Macclesfield (part of the Hundred) known as the Halmote Court was held monthly in the courthouse at Macclesfield.

The date when man first settled in Macclesfield will never be known, but there is evidence in abundance that ancient man lived in and around.

Stone Age Sites

An eminent historian, archaeologist and geologist, Dr J.D.Sainter in his book *Scientific Ramblings around Macclesfield* published in 1878 tells us that behind Mount Pleasant, Prestbury Road, there was to be seen a tumulus (a man-made mound) which, when explored, yielded a Neolithic or later Stone Age burial. At the foot of this mound, westward, there were the remains of a peat bog and an oblong block of greenstone, weighing 25 lbs, was taken out of it that had been used by the Ancient Britons as a grinding stone.

The barrow was described as being 30 yards in diameter at the base and 25 feet high. 15 feet in thickness of earth had been added to form a barrow. When the soil was removed, human bones were discovered and a highly polished flint saw with a very fine serrated edge. It is believed it could have been a Chieftain's burial ground.

Dr Sainter went on to say that there appeared to have been a Celtic settlement around the Prestbury Road area (where the cemetery now is) dating to before the arrival of the Romans in this country.

Quern

Hand grain rubber, Cemetery

Limestone hammer, Dane Moss

Dr Whitaker in his *History of Manchester*, also published in the 19th century, tells us on September 27,1871, a tumulus was opened on the Macclesfield Common which contained charcoal ashes and a few remains of burnt bones. There are, literally, dozens of other burial sites in the area that will yield valuable historical data when excavated.

On Danes Moss, that sad-looking area of peat moss south of Macclesfield, relics of bygone ages have been disentombed which, they had been more carefully excavated, would have contributed even more interesting facts. Unearthed have been swords, iron spear heads and an ancient iron bow. The Stoke-on-Trent Museum possessed two 'querns' which were found on Danes Moss when the railway was being cut through. They were of rude workmanship and certainly dated from a very remote period. The quern is a hand-mill for parched or burnt corn; it consists of two portable stones, the lower one on a cylinder, with a basin formed in it at the top. An upper stone was fitted into this and the corn was ground between them. The flour ran out of the sides.

Other evidence of early man has been found at the present cemetery. It has been identified by the British Museum as a net-weight or net-sinker and is said to be of a very early date.

Two miles out of Macclesfield, at Butley, there was discovered what Ormerod in his *History of Cheshire* refers to as an "ancient cemetery". A cinerary urn was found, containing burnt bones in a cairn and this was surrounded by other cairns, although how many is not mentioned. The urn would probably have contained the ashes of some person of note and surrounding cairns would be for his servants or slaves, or perhaps his wife.

There are many more records of burial grounds being found in and around Macclesfield. There is one at Tytherington, now in the middle of housing estate and the area of bleak land known as Macclesfield Forest contains much evidence of ancient man in the form of carved stones and burial grounds. An urn and arrow heads were found at Langley and flint arrow heads and a knife at the stone circle at Clulow Cross. Place names give further clues - for example Blakelow, near the golf course, denotes a burial ground.

The Romans

And what about the Romans? It is unlikely that our town was of much importance to these invaders, although in the neighbourhood of Macclesfield there are still to be seen traces of Roman occupation. And as Macclesfield is so close to the Roman towns or cities of Manchester, Warrington and Chester (not to mention the Spa Town of Buxton) it is highly likely there would have been some activity here associated with the Romans.

Roman legions stayed only 12 miles away in Buxton over a period of 400 years and a Roman road, later a packhorse trail for the salt carriers, passes down the steep hill in Saltersford leading to Jenkin Chapel - well defined traces of it may be seen today crossing the top of the path to Pym Chair. It is thought that this is a part of Ermine Street from Mancunium to Buxton by way of Stockport and Bramhall. Another Roman road has been identified which went through Twemlow, Withington, Chelford, Capesthorne, Henbury, Birtles, Butley, Bollington and Rainow, where, at the foot of Pike Low it is thought to have joined the Ermine Street road.

J.P.Earwaker of Merton College, Oxford in his 1880s work *East Cheshire* mentions a discovery of Roman remains at Astle Park near Chelford and said there were indications of a Roman road from Henbury to Chelford. And of course the Romans worked the Alderley Edge copper mines. Could slave labour have come from Macclesfield? A number of historians have classed the earthworks at Toot Hill, on the edge of Macclesfield Forest as Roman - for example, Mr John Earles described the workings as a Roman camp. There is some evidence for this from the name - Toot, or Teut, is the Latin for Mercury - the god who guarded travellers. Others, however, connect it more with a hunting enclosure in the Forest, from which animals would be released for the chase. I subscribe to this theory.

During the construction of the Macclesfield Cemetery and when the railway was being built through Macclesfield, many interesting discoveries were made, particularly the remains of wild horses, wild boar and a quantity of Roman coin. There is also undocumented evidence that a quantity of Roman coins were found in the bed of the River Bollin near Waters Green.

In the year 410 the Romans left Britain and the British, so accustomed to being defended by the Legions, fell easy prey to attackers. The Angles formed the Kingdom of Mercia which included the district around Macclesfield.

An Occupied Town

During Macclesfield's occupation by the Angles and Saxons, a hall for the Saxon earls was built on the southwest of the town, in what is now called Ryles Park. It had a large and well-stocked deer park extending for many miles. This mansion was a residence for the Earls of Mercia for centuries. Penda, king of Mercia, erected the Anglo Saxon stones in Sandbach market place and there is no doubt this famous king stayed in his manor house at Macclesfield on occasions, undoubtedly to hunt: the deer in his parklands or the wolf and wild boar in Macclesfield Forest.

Gentlemen at a hunting lodge in Macclesfield Forest at the turn of the century. The lands of Macclesfield Forest have been used as the domain of the hunter - from Kings of England to the poorest of poachers - throughout the centuries.

Later, the Normans were to construct a mansion on the same spot but the Saxon one would have consisted of an irregular group of buildings and, in the centre of these, would be a hall and beyond, a round tower - the stronghold of the whole residence and a chapel (the church of St Allowes, now St Michael's was founded 300 years later although there may have been a pagan temple at the spot where our Parish Church now is. At this period it would undoubtedly have been converted to a Christian site). A fragment of a

Tossing a coin for the best shooting positions at Macclesfield Forest, circa 1912.

Saxon cross was discovered in the course of the restoration of St Michael's in 1898. It was unearthed from beneath a wall in the Legh Chapel. No doubt the chapels at Ryles Park and in the Market Place, and also at Prestbury, were connected by virtue of intermixing clergy.

There is a fine Runic stone at Prestbury Church. For many centuries it was concealed within the walls of the church and was only rediscovered during alterations to the fabric.

Macclesfield Parish Church. This picture was taken
about the turn of the century. Was there a church
on this site before the present structure - and was it
the site of a pagan temple before Christianity came
to these isles?

It is supposed to be a very ancient Saxon monument erected to commemorate the introduction of Christianity among the pagan inhabitants of these parts. The Saxon stones now in West Park came originally from the Forest; another stands at Clulow Cross.

The Norman Invasion

At the time of the Norman invasion, Macclesfield was under the rule of Edwin, Earl of Mercia, who was grandson of the renowned Leofric and his grandmother was the famous Lady Godiva. Algar succeeded Leofric as Earl and his two sons were Edwin and Morcar. Edwin became Earl of Mercia and Morcar, Earl of Northumberland at their father's death. These two brothers were among the last of the Anglo Saxons to struggle against Norman domination. Hereward the Wake was their famous uncle.

Edwin and Morcar fought at the Battle of Hastings and, when defeated, retired to London and attempted to rally their scattered forces - including their Macclesfield soldiers. When William the Conqueror advanced to London, Edwin withdrew his forces to Mercia and defied William who, recognising Edwin's power, sought to propitiate him by promising him the hand of his daughter, Adelaide. But the Norman nobles objected to her marrying a Saxon, so William went back on his promise. As a result, Edwin and Morcar rose in rebellion but were defeated; the lands of the Saxon earls were confiscated and divided among the Norman nobles, the domain and hall at Macclesfield becoming the property of the Earl of Chester - the Conqueror's nephew, Hugh.

To make matters worse, the entire area of Macclesfield and district was laid to waste by the Normans with fire and sword. It is highly probable that Macclesfield's church was destroyed along with the church at Prestbury. The Domesday survey describes Macclesfield as being a "waste". It had been worth eight pounds - big money in those days - but was now only worth 20 shillings.

Domesday

In the Domesday Survey (which was finished in 1086) the return for Macclesfield Hundred (referred to as the old 'Hameston') is a very full one. The whole of the County of Chester had been granted to Hugh Lupus, the first Norman Earl of Chester, by the Conqueror, and the greater part of the land was held by him except in those cases where he had granted it away to his Norman followers or had confirmed a few of the Saxon noblemen in their old possessions.

The Domesday entry reads: "The Earl (of Chester) himself holds MACLESFIELD (Macclesfield). Earl Edwin held it. (There are) four serfs. There are two hides rateable to the gelt. The land is ten carucates. One is in the demesne, and there is a mill to supply the Hall. There is a wood six leagues long and four broad. There were seven hays, and there is a meadow for oxen. The third penny of the Hundred belongs to this manor. In King Edward's time it was worth eight pounds, now twenty shillings. It was waste".

The "hide" and "carucate" were measures of land, generally ploughed or cultivated, varying in quantity in different districts. A hide is generally 100-150 acres, while a carucate was as much as a team of oxen could plough in one year. The "gelt" was a land tax and a "league" was a mile and a half. A "hay" was a deer fence or enclosure. We still have Whalley Hays and Lower Hays and Arborhay in Macclesfield.

Hugh Lupus , Earl of Chester and his successors held Macclesfield until 1237 when the estate became the property of the Crown and was then held by the Prince of Wales, or the reigning sovereigns, as Earls of Chester.

Hugh - known as Hugh the Wolf - was a stern and ruthless baron and he erected strong fortresses in various parts of Cheshire, one of which was built on site of the hall of the Earls of Chester at Ryles Park. No traces of this remain but, in the Congleton Road area of Macclesfield, there was once a field called "Castle Field". The castle would have been surrounded by a moat or ditch and the walls of the keep could have been 15 feet thick.

Macclesfield Forest and Robin Hood

There can be little doubt the Norman and Plantagenet kings frequently visited the powerful and influential Earls of Chester at the Macclesfield castle and indulged in hunting and hawking in the park and forest. The severe forest laws that applied to Macclesfield Forest and others were there to keep the game for the rich to kill, not the poor to eat, and the killing of a deer or even a hare was punishable by death. But, in spite if this, a lot of poaching went on and the forests, including Macclesfield, became the haunts of outlaws. One of the most famous is, of course, Robin Hood and his Merry Men who have many associates with the area - note, for example, the Robin Hood pub at Rainow.

The Forest of Macclesfield - not the man made, uniform, forest created by the Water Board that passes for a forest today - was extensive. It was not, in the main, trees, but wild land. It covered most of the area between Macclesfield, Buxton and Leek and stretched north to Stockport. Indeed, there was connecting woodland stretching all the way to the east coast of England, which incorporated Sherwood.

It is said that Will Scarlett, a prominent member of Robin's forest outlaws, was a native of Macclesfield. In an old English ballad, Robin is mentioned with Ranulph, the Earl of

Chester (who owned Macclesfield Forest) and Will Scarlett says, in the rhyme, "In Maxfelde town I was born and bred".

It is interesting that Robin Hood, according to legend, was the Earl of Huntingdon. In Robin Hood's time the Earl of Huntingdon was David St Liz who married the daughter of the Earl of Chester.

Robin and the Stranger -

a ballad concerning Macclesfield, from the time of Edward II

The poem starts with Robin meeting a young man wearing a silk doublet and scarlet stockings. They fight and Robin asks who he is and where he is from:

The stranger then answered bold Robin Hood,
"I'll tell thee where I do dwell:
In Maxfield town I was born,
My name is young Gamwell.
For killing of my own father's steward
I am forced to this English wood,
And for to seek an uncle of mine,
Some call him Robin Hood."
"But art thou a cousin of Robin Hood then?
The sooner we should have done."
"As I hope to be saved," the stranger then said ,
"I am his own sister's son."

The ballad continues and, eventually, a beautiful damsel comes along, riding a black palfrey. Her rose-like cheeks deepen in hue when she sees the outlaws and her face wears an expression of sorrow. Robin questions her, and she says she has come from London which is besieged by the Prince of Arragon who, with two giants, challenges any three to combat, swearing he will have the princess or he will lay waste to the land.

"When is this day?" quoth Robin Hood,
"Tell me this and no more."
"On midsummer next" the damsel said,
"Which is June the twentyfour."

Robin, Will and Little John set off for London disguised as pilgrims from the Holy

Land and, needless to say, they defeat the giants. The King grants Robin and his men a pardon and the princess then takes Will by the hand saying: "Here I make my choice".

> With that a noble lord stept forth,
> Of Maxfield earl was he,
> Who looked Will Scarlet in the face
> And wept most bitterly.
> Quoth he, "I had a son like thee,
> Whom I loved wondrous well;
> But he is gone or rather dead:
> His name is young Gamwell."
> Then did Will Scarlet fall on his knees,
> Cried "Father! father! here
> Here kneels your son, your young Gamwell,
> Who said you loved so dear!"

Borough Charter

A charter was granted to the Borough of Macclesfield by Ranulf, Earl of Chester, and tradition - but not fact - has it that this was in 1220. The charter involved 120 Macclesfield men who received some kind of freedom in return for a yearly payment of twelve silver pennies.

When the seventh earl of Chester, John Scott, died in 1238 he had only two daughters and , so, the Crown took the earldom. King Henry III gave the earldom and the manor and forest of Macclesfield to his son, Prince Edward, afterwards Edward Ist.By 1261, Macclesfield was incorporated as a free borough thanks to Edward who granted to the residents of Macclesfield freedom from various dues demanded and collected by the local authorities.

But the Prince, however, while generous in giving the burgesses exemptions from local "taxes" was not unmindful of the royal purse. He made sure the "beloved burgesses" had to grind their corn at his mill in Macclesfield and to bake their bread in his ovens.

Edward and his consort, Eleanor, made several visits to Macclesfield and stayed at the manor or castle in the park. Between the years 1277-84 the king visited the town at least once a year while the conquest of Wales was at its height. Archers from Macclesfield were used in his battles.

At the same time as granting the royal privileges, the heir apparent to the English throne conferred the town upon his consort. She founded the church on its present site in

Macclesfield's old Church from a 17th century print.

1278. The consecration service was performed by the Bishop of St Asaph who acted for the Bishop of Lichfield and Coventry in whose diocese Macclesfield was until the creation of the see of Chester in 1541 (note the connection, still, that remained with the old Mercian area through the Bishop of Lichfield). Unfortunately, no records remain of what must have been a very imposing ceremony and one memento only of the occasion is left to us - a cross cut in stone - which may still be seen near the entrance to the Legh Chapel.

The Young Pretender

December 1st, 1745, was the day when Bonny Prince Charlie - Prince Charles Edward Stuart - came to town, along with 6,500 men. His intention was to march to London in support of his claim for the throne against the Hanoverian King of England, George II. The Young Pretender and his father, James, were both Roman Catholic - the main factor which prevented their crowning, although their royal blood was more direct than George's.

Having come south from Scotland, the 6,000 men and boys and about 500 cavalry bedraggled and tired, stopped in the town and set about cleaning their weapons.

What a terrifying sight this must have been for the inhabitants, who had been warned of the impending arrival by a vanguard who had arrived the day before and distributed leaflets from the market cross. The Macclesfield people sent Samson Salt (a good Cheshire name) to Stockport to get news of the army but he was captured on his way.

Most of the people of the town were in church on Sunday morning, presumably praying, when they heard the sound of the approaching army which had come in two parts, one via Stockport and the other via Alderley Edge. Many of the townfolk hastily fled town, clutching their valuables.

The army arrived at mid-day and the quartermasters asked where Sir Peter Davenport's house was. Sir Peter was an ancestor of Sir Walter Bromley Davenport of Capesthorne Hall, and he had a town house in King Edward Street, at that time called Back Lane. It is assumed that the Prince thought he would be helped by Sir Peter, but the gentleman was not in Macclesfield at the time and so the front door of his house was marked by Prince Charles' men with the word "Prince". It appears that Sir Peter later got into trouble for being known by the Prince and for staying at his home (albeit, when he was not there), for the following year his house was vacated and, in 1748, it was converted to the King Edward the Sixth Grammar School and the street changed from Back Lane to King Edward street.

When the Prince arrived, an order went to the Mayor, Thomas Cooper, to attend with his aldermen and officers at the market cross to proclaim the Pretender King of England. The Mayor did so, obviously fearing for his life, and a peal of bells was rung from the church for fear of being accused of an insult, but in the confusion the peal was rung backwards. The poor Mayor tried to raise a "hooray" from the onlookers but they "stood in silence with horror and consternation on their faces". The army of 6,000 plus was billetted all over the town in the taverns and inns and private homes. Everywhere the soldiers stayed had to be kept illuminated all night.

Some of the soldiers stayed at the Sun Inn in Chestergate (where the Natwest Bank now stands). This was the favourite hangout of a well known crook called Joseph Clarke and, during the night, for whatever reason, he got into a fight with a Scottish soldier. He took a sword from the hands of the soldier and killed him then made his escape. So enraged were the soldiers that they threatened to set fire to the town unless the culprit was given up, but no-one admitted to knowing his whereabouts.

Five years later, incidentally, Clarke slew a man who was sent to arrest him on a charge of deer slaying at Shrigley Hall.

Several officers were billetted at the house of Mr John Stafford, a lawyer, at the corner of Jordangate and Cumberland Street. Women and boys lying in his barn on straw "like a

THE OLD SUN INN

A famous Macclesfield hostelry which formerly stood in Chestergate on the site of Parr's Bank Buildings and the Post Office, adjoining the house (itself one of the oldest buildings in the town).

kennel of hounds, some of 'em stark naked." On discovering the army was to stay for another day, John Stafford took his wife and "a great train of other females" to Shrigley Hall.

Prince Charles and his men left on Tuesday, December 3rd, having stolen, or commandeered, all the arms and ammunition they could find in the town. They forced the Macclesfield bakers to bake wagon loads of bread. The Prince had demanded money from the town, claiming his right as the natural king to the local taxes, which amounted to £35 17s 2$\frac{1}{2}$d. Later, the Collectors of Excise petitioned the Treasury, saying the people of Macclesfield had been forced to pay this to the army and should not be made to pay a second time.

The Pretender then arrived in Leek. They travelled two groups - one via Congleton and the other on the old Macclesfield to Leek road which went through Wincle, past the Ship Inn. They went on through Ashbourne and, when they reached, Derby decided to retreat.

On the way to Leek, a drummer in the army of the Scots sat on an outcrop on Bosley Cloud. A sniper from the Cheshire Dragoons killed him as he was seated there, playing his drum. That outcrop, near to the Congleton Road, is now known as Drummer's Knob.

When the Rebels left Macclesfield there was undoubtedly some celebration taking place but, when news reached the Town that he was returning, the jubilation would quickly have turned to panic. On the night of Friday, December 6th, a messenger was sent to Leek and he returned the following day to say that they would arrive the next day. Most of the civic worthies, including the Mayor, fled the town, and those who stayed behind barricaded their homes. The main part of the army arrived on Sunday, December 8th, although the Prince himself did not return to the town - he went over the Leek moors to Manchester and the small inn where he stayed the night is now called Royal Cottage.

Macclesfield was plundered and anything of value was stolen. The rebels discovered that there was money from a subscription held in support of the government and they demanded this cash by six a.m. the following day or the town would be burned down. They threatened the Mayoress (yes, the Mayor had left her behind!) but she denied any knowledge of it. The Town Clerk produced a copy of the subscription list and those who had given money were made to give the rebels an equal amount of money. The bedraggled army left on December 9th and went northwards.

The events described so far are largely thanks to the later writings of our lawyer friend, Mr Stafford. But there is another account of the army's stay in Macclesfield.

In a book "A Complete History of the Rebellion of 1745, from its rise to its total suppression at the glorious Battle of Culloden in April, 1746," by James Kay, the author followed the army into Macclesfield. He says that as the army was marching out of Macclesfield, one of them wanted to buy a cap. He was shown to a shop by a deserter from the King's Army, who drew a dirk from the Scotsman's side and stabbed him in the thigh. He ran through the Angel Inn and made his escape. Some of the army returned and threatened to burn the town unless the offender was handed over. As he could not be found, the landlord of the Angel and the owner the house next to the shop where the stabbing took place were carried away as hostages.

The author, James Kay was something of a "James Bond" character it would seem, for he arrived in town at this time thinking the army had left. They recognised him as a spy and he ran off. He went to the Mayor who advised him to stay at the Angel. He did so and put his arms and bullets in the bed for safety. These were highland pistols and he also had a highland sword. A maid, when making his bed, reported that some of the rebels had left their arms. However, the confusion was explained.

The Duke of Cumberland and his army came northward and caused the Scots to retreat from Derby. The Duke's army eventually arrived in Macclesfield and here hanged a deserter they had picked up along the way. He was hanged from the Guild Hall steps and surgeon purchased the body for 4s 6d, intending to use it for anatomical purposes. Eventually it was buried at Gawsworth.

The house at the corner of Jordangate owned by lawyer Stafford accommodated the Duke during his stay and was henceforth known as Cumberland House.

2 The Silk Trade

Buttonmen and Flashmen

There is no doubt that people from within the township of Macclesfield went up to the moorland to farm because there is a record of three - Ralph Simpson, Edward Shaw and George Brocklehurst "all of Macclesfield" renting land.

What is of more interest is the fact that their occupations were given as "button men" --- one of the first references to the trade or craft of button making which had grown in Macclesfield.

Ray, in his *History of the Rebellion* which was published in 1749 had mentioned that Macclesfield's chief manufacturing industry was buttons, but it is evident this had come about a long time before, for in the *History of the County Round Manchester in 1795* the author said that silk buttons had been in use for two centuries and mills had been erected at both Macclesfield and Stockport "long ago" for winding silk and making twist for buttons.

In the book *Swythamley and its Neighbourhood* published by Sir Philip Lancaster Brocklehurst in 1874, there is reference to gangs of men who, in the 18th century, lived around the wild country around Three Shire Heads where Cheshire, Staffordshire and Derbyshire meet. These characters were known as the Flash Men after the village of Flash. They were pedlars of silk buttons but, over the years, they became a gang of violent criminals who, among other misdeeds, became very proficient counterfeiters.

CONVICTION OF
SILK STEALERS AND RECEIVERS.
AT KNUTSFORD SESSIONS.

(Re-printed from the Macclesfield Courier and Herald, December 3rd, 1864.)

Silk stealers and receivers take considerable pains, and from time to time have displayed some ingenuity, in devising means to evade detection and give to their nefarious doings the outside appearance of honest dealing. From the annals of our local police courts, and the records of Assizes and Sessions, as regularly chronicled in our columns, might be collated a catalogue of contrivances resorted to for this purpose, that would be amusing for their ingenuity were it not for the rascality of their design; and it is not a little remarkable that in every instance the rogue has been convicted chiefly on the evidence of his own invention. It has fallen to our lot, as chroniclers of passing events, to tell of bed pillows stuffed, not with the feathery down of the Eider duck, but with the more costly production of the silk worm, stowed away beneath the folds of sheet and blanket as the least likely place in which a policeman would expect to find stolen property. We have a vivid recollection of that naughty housewife who was accosted a short time ago in a certain thoroughfare not a hundred miles from Watersgreen, by one of our borough constables, who politely escorted her to the police office, and caused her unceremoniously to be divested of a crinoline whose expansiveness rested not so much on steel hoops, as on a series of capacious pockets filled with purloined silk; which act condemned her lord and master in the sum of £20 and costs, and forfeiture of the silk. Our memory turns to the ingenious manner in which another dabbler in pilfered goods, fitted up the space intervening between the flooring of one room and the ceiling of another room, with all the appliances of a warehouse, and filled it with his ill-gotten gains, until the rude hand of a detective officer brought the hidden receptacle to light, and the guilty one was mulcted in the penalty of £20 and expences, and forfeiture of the silk. Equally ingenious, in its way, was the machinery discovered in the chimney of a house not a stone's throw from the river Bollin, where a policeman pulling a nail out of the wall over a mantle piece, pulled with it a string, working on a pully and attached in the dust pipe to a bag containing unmanufactured silk, which, by being let down and drawn up, like the bucket of a well, could be reached under the empty grate and filled or emptied as the case might require. Men's hats have been unexpectedly taken off, and found to contain something more than the *crania* of their wearers. Factory operatives have gone to their mills like Pharoah's lean kine, and returned like the Egyptian monarch's fat kine, suddenly corpulent of Italian organzine, and as suddenly reduced to normal proportion on gaining the parlours of those human spiders known as receivers of stolen goods, commonly called by the *soubriquet* of Turkey Merchants. Everybody in Macclesfield has heard of the celebrated beer barrel which ran Bass's pale ale at one end and Bengal tram at the other. A glance over the file of the *Courier* tells us of a certain dwelling in Bank-street where stolen silk was found in the roof; another tenement in Lunt-hill had a neatly-constructed box fitted up in the staircase; and the wife of a weaver in Townley-street hid her stolen booty in the oven. Only the other day a cabbage garden was found prolific of silk bobbins, and a rabbit cote converted into a receptacle for stolen silk, constructed in a manner described in the report given in another part of our paper of the trial and conviction of its proprietor—a man who not many months ago travelled from Macclesfield to Knutsford to speak to the good character of a confederate then on his trial, and in twenty-four hours afterwards wearing a convict's livery for a precisely similar offence to that of which he himself has also been convicted and sentenced to five years' penal servitude at the hulks.

If the case of Samuel Sidebottom stood alone, there might be cause for congratulation that among the many thousands employed in the silk trade in this town, so few cases of dishonesty are brought to light; but there is too much reason to fear that the instances cropping out now and then in our police courts are only the index of a secret system of wholesale plundering yet remaining undiscovered. Let those lending themselves to such dishonesty take warning before it is too late, for as sure as water finds its own level, so sure will cowardly depredations like these recoil on the heads of the perpetrators. The highwayman, who boldly demands "your bullion or your brains," is a hero compared with the slinking thief-trainer who lacks the courage to do what he too often succeeds in inveigling others to do, for a gain trifling in amount in proportion to with what he himself often realises.

The very means which Sidebottom employed to escape detection led to his conviction. At the trial, even his counsel, one of the ablest and most ingenious advocates on the circuit, evidently felt that his client had woven round himself a web from the meshes of which forensic eloquence could not rescue him. Had there been a loophole, Mr. Horatio Lloyd was just the man to drag him through it; but there was not a chink in the evidence affording the faintest glimmer of hope. All that the learned counsel asked was, the benefit of a doubt; the Court and the Jury said there was no doubt, and so will every one say who reads the case in our Sessions report. Our object in drawing attention to the case, is to point out the severe punishment awaiting those convicted of stealing and receiving silk. A few years ago, Sidebottom would have been put in the witness box, to give evidence against the thieves, rather than have been arraigned in the felon's dock. But the law relating to this offence has happily changed. Sidebottom stood convicted on the statements of his own victims as well as on the evidence of his own acts, and in his old age has brought upon himself a punishment which he richly deserves. If there are any of her Majesty's lieges in Macclesfield still sleeping on Yuen-fa, or owning beer-barrels running Burton XX or China three-threads at the will of the tapster; if there are still chimneys crammed with Tsatlee, rabbits fed on Taysaam, and cabbage beds yielding Bengal raw silk, the proprietors thereof may take this as a warning that the sooner they abandon such dangerous property the better. Over and over again has the Court of Quarter Sessions expressed its determination to visit such cases with the utmost rigour of the law, and it has not been slow to give effect to this determination. Society demands, the law provides, the Court awards that an example should be made of such men, and public opinion will endorse the sentence passed at Knutsford on Wednesday last. The prisoner carries his grey hairs into penal servitude, there to languish with those of his confederates whose sins, like his, found them out; and if his case should have the desired effect of deterring others from acting likewise,—if it acts as a warning to those who, for a paltry bribe, consent to plunder the very persons on whose prosperity their own welfare depends, and whom the common instincts of nature should lead them to protect,—if the salutary lesson is learnt that honesty is the best policy, then Samuel Sidebottom and his accomplices will not have suffered in vain.

This lawless gang, The Flashmen, who had originally been sellers and manufacturers of button, took advantage of their knowledge of button manufacturing to make coins! They were familiar with the machinery needed to mould and stamp buttons and adapted it for the manufacture of base coins.

The Flashmen lived all over the neighbourhood above Macclesfield, and there is a legend that they took advantage of Three Shire Heads where the three counties meet, avoiding capture simply by stepping from one county into the next. So wild and so bleak was the area, that the former button makers turned coiners carried on their illegal deeds more or less with impunity. They would journey into Macclesfield, Leek and Buxton and pass their coins to tradespeople and others they duped.

Their headquarters was Meg Lane Farm, Higher Sutton, and some of the coin machines they used were still, I believe, kept there until recently. It was from Meg Lane Farm that the gang was eventually found after being betrayed by a young girl who lived with one of the gang at a lonely farmhouse. On the information she laid with the authorities, the gang was eventually broken up and they were hanged at Chester. Records at Chester have failed to reveal any such hangings, but hangings in those times were so frequent that it is quite likely many were either recorded briefly or not at all.

Once, there was a tale of Macclesfield Forest entitled *Spellbound* by a writer who used the pen name of Red Girdle. One chapter, headed "The Forest Fay" tells the story of the Meg Lane Gang and , in particular, one of the members of the Flashmen known as "Black Hugh Raven".

Black Hugh is described as, when being angry, a formidable fellow. "His teeth gnashed and the fire from his eyeballs flashed." He was responsible for lighting beacons on Hollinsclough to warn the gang of pending danger.

The story says of Meg Lane:
"South East of Hollins you may trace
An old, a lone, and a sullen place
Hid in the gloomy woods that grow
Throughout the glen that lies below.
Who wills a nearer view to gain
Must thread a dark and narrow lane;
Entered by passing through a wood,
And o'er the mill stream's murmuring flood.
Here shrubs run wild and hedges high
And meeting trees obscure the sky;
And bats and owls in autumn night,

Indulge secure their lonely flight.
At this lane and there stands alone
The gloomy house all built of stone
Thick rugged walls of dark grey rock,
skill, taste and time alike do mock;
The narrow houses for windows made
To let in light seem half afraid."

It was here that Black Hugh dwelt with his sole companions, two men "as wild as fierce as Hugh", and two dogs called "Rock" and "Chase". The writer tells of a secret cavern in which were hid the hoards of cups, flagons, "pieces of rich and costly plate which nobles used in times of state" and of the furnace in which the metal was melted down."

After the gang was caught, the farmhouse passed into other hands but many years later, in cleaning out a well in the farmyard, various implements were found, among them a powerful coining machine worked by a screw for punching out the coins. These implements were made by a man named Isaac Heath who kept a smithy where the Ryles Arms is now situated in Hollins Lane. They were, for many years, in the possession of Mr William Whiston, J.P., of Langley.

The Button Trade

There is a possibility that button making took place in Macclesfield as early as the fourteenth century, but the first written record is in 1574 in the town's accounts for "Buttons and for making buttons" and, that year, the mayor and burgesses, or the town council, passed an order that no strangers could engage in button making, thus ensuring Maxonians had the monopoly sewn up. What this also did was to keep strangers out of Macclesfield -- strangers who could bring with them disease, especially from London. In 1604 the town prohibited any "foreigner" to settle and anyone who harboured a stranger was liable to imprisonment. Sixty years later two persons in every street in Macclesfield were chosen "to enquire and take account" of anyone who was not from Macclesfield. This particularly referred to the people who brought silk from London, from which the buttons were made. All types of disease, primarily, the plague were rife in the capital but other "social" diseases came with these people also.

The Corporation decided, in 1698, to erect its first workhouse and house of correction wherein "poor children and other poor that are fit ... be set to button making".

When the Huguenots - French Protestants who fled from France - settled in London, they became famous for silk weaving. The area of London they lived in was called Spitalfields and an area of Macclesfield became known as Spitalfields, also, because of the connection between Macclesfield and the Huguenots. Much of their thrown silk was sent from Macclesfield. It later became known as Prospect Buildings and the passage that once led to the now demolished area off Mill Street is still there.

It is evident, therefore, that button making was organised in Macclesfield during the 1600s. Originally the silk or mohair was twisted around wooden moulds by women and children, mainly in their own homes, using a needle. But, as our Flash Coiners showed, the button foundations became metal, and no doubt the menfolk were engaged in manufacturing these.

By the time Bonny Prince Charlie visited town, the chief industry was certainly button making and many people from the country areas had been attracted into town by the promise of more work and more pay than they could get from farming.

The Flashmen had been the original hawkers of these buttons and this was the main source of sale (although, it should be said, there were many honest sellers of buttons as well). They would visit the weekly markets and the annual fairs throughout the North West and the Midlands. By the eighteenth century, the London merchants were handling the Macclesfield buttons and selling them through the United Kingdom and in Europe and America, not to mention Russia.

Raw silk needs to be prepared and twisted , and this was - to a great extent - done in Macclesfield. From the production of thread for buttons grew the preparation of thread for other items and, from this, Macclesfield's silk industry developed. The Huguenots, who settled in London in 1688 wove silk in London and silk thread for their looms came from, among other towns, Macclesfield.

From a cottage industry, where mothers and daughters would wind the silken thread around the button moulds made by father (who probably hawked the buttons at market as well) grew the industry that made Macclesfield famous. Just when people began to congregate to manufacture their wares is not certain. Perhaps the first "co-operative factories" were merely one or two families working together in a biggish house. Throwing houses, where throwsters (the workers who twisted the silk strands into thread) worked together, became necessary because of the demand for space and for storing the valuable raw material. The odds and ends left over from manufacture, were made up into sewing silk, knee garters, tassles and fringes and in 1765 it was estimated that up to 15,000 people were employed in "salvaging" the waste.

This did not refer, I believe, entirely to Macclesfield but to neighbouring towns and villages as well -- the largest town being Leek.

The population of Macclesfield grew and the first census, although not an official one, took place in May of 1787. It showed the township contained 1412 inhabited houses and a population of 6794, not taking into account the neighbouring townships of Hurdsfield and Sutton (around the Mill Lane area) which today we look upon as part of Macclesfield.

The following is the record:

	Houses	Inhabitants
Watercotes	131	650
Park green	76	402
Sunderland Street, Townley Street and Sugar street	124	599
The Waters	328	1570
Newgate	20	106
Mill Street	102	472
Dog Lane	65	260
The Gutters, Church Side, Goose Lane	98	408
Barn Street	136	679
Chestergate	125	611
Back Street, Little Street	117	586
Jordangate	90	451

The document also shows there were 56 boarders at the Grammar School in King Edward Street and about 50 inmates of the Poor House. It clearly shows how many were crowded into the houses in The Waters -- far more than any other part of Town.

The first official census was in 1801 and this shows that in the space of 14 years the population had swelled to 8,743. This doubled in the next 20 years and, by the 1851 census had doubled again. The Hurdsfield and Sutton townships grew at an equal rate and, what had once been green fields between Macclesfield, Hurdsfield and Sutton, was now completely built up. Macclesfield, swallowed up these two villages. The new Borough contained, in 1851, 39,048 people.

In Mr John Corry's *History of Macclesfield* we are informed that in the year 1775 the wages paid to millmen and stewards were seven shillings a week; women employed as doublers and twisters received three shillings and six pence a week. Children employed as silk piercers were hired for three years at the rate of sixpence a week for the first year and ninepence and a shilling a week , respectively, for the two following. Of course, these prices must be looked at relative to the purchasing power of the day. Fresh butter could be bought in the Macclesfield market for four pence a 1 lb; the best Macclesfield Cheshire cheese cost two pence a pound. Brown bread was sold for five farthings a pound, fine flour cost a shilling a peck and milk could be bought for a penny a quart.

Charles Roe (1715-1781)

Charles Roe, who built the first mill in Macclesfield used for the throwing of silk. It was at the bottom of Mill Street at the junction with Park Green. A modern building, called Silk House, now stands on the site.

Undoubtedly, the one person who, more than any other, made Macclesfield famous was Charles Roe. The house where he lived has been preserved and stands at the corner of Chestergate and Churchill Way as a monument to him although the house, a listed building of special architectural and historical interest, was built around 1670. At that time, it was on land on the outskirts of town and it is not known who lived there until Charles Roe moved in during the mid-18th century.

But much more is known about its famous owner --probably the most famous of Macclesfield's historical figures. He was an industrial pioneer, a shrewd businessman, a freeman of the borough and contributed to many aspects of the town's social and religious life.

Roe was born in Castleton, Derbyshire, the son of a clergyman. A brother of his became a curate in Macclesfield in 1724 and Charles followed him. He worked in Macclesfield as a merchant for the silk button industry, (then at its peak) and perfected a machine for throwing raw silk by means of a waterwheel. By 1762 he is recorded as having the fourth largest silk throwsters in Macclesfield but he sold his shares in the silk business by 1764 when his shrewd business sense told him of the slump that would result in the industry after the Seven Years' War with France. He gambled correctly because soon after he sold out the firm fell on hard times and went bankrupt.

In 1758, he and his brother-in-law obtained permission to build a copper smelting works on Macclesfield Common, which soon expanded. He later opened works in Bosley and Eaton. Copper Street, Brasshouse Street and Smelthouses bear witness to this industry. The ore came from, at one time, Alderley Edge, and the Lake District. During a holiday in Wales, he discovered a copper mine in Anglesey which he purchased.

He became convinced of the importance of cheap transport and he supported and sponsored an ambitious scheme for a Macclesfield canal. However, owing to the intention of the Duke of Bridgewater, whose Bridgewater Canal was to be a prominent means of transport, a bill for the introduction of the Macclesfield Canal was defeated in the House of Lords in 1766 and was eventually shelved for a number of years. Roe was Mayor in 1747 and 48 and he also made an important contribution to the religious life of the town. He was concerned about the impact Methodism was having and decided to build Christ Church, bearing the £6,000 building costs himself.

He appointed the famous preacher with Wesleyan sympathies, the Rev David Simpson, as vicar and it was at Christ Church that he was buried in May, 1781 "a much feared and much loved man".

At Charles Roe's copper works, between the Smelthouses and the Brasshouses, was a large windmill which was used for grinding the ore. This structure gave its name to Windmill Brow and Windmill Square - not to mention Windmill Street. Many years afterwards it was pulled down and re-erected at Kerridge where it remained until the Second World War. At this time it was demolished again and the stone was taken to Burtonwood where it was used as a foundation for the American Airforce runway.

Roe was married three times and had four children by his first wife, eight by his second and one by his third, who survived him by over 30 years and eventually left her sedan chair to the town --to carry the poor to the workhouse!

Rise and Fall of the Silk Industry

The weaving of silk was introduced into the town of Macclesfield in or around the year 1790 when a Huguenot refugee, Margaret Moburn, was brought to a workshop in Back Street along with several other people from London. Margaret was induced to join the employment of James Pearson and to teach weaving and warping to his employees in a weaving shed in Sunderland Street. Margaret co-habited with James for a number of years.

Houses were built especially to accommodate hand loom weavers. Long rows of windows on the upper storey were especially to let in as much light as possible and there are still quite a few houses in Macclesfield that once were used as "cottage industry", with the family living on the first floors and the mother and father working on the top. here, in an extremely rare photograph, can be seen two of the very last home weavers in Macclesfield, working from their home in the Elizabeth Street area of town.

The war between England and France (1793-1815) meant French silk was scarce and this was an undoubted boost for Macclesfield. Mills flourished in the town, and people came from far and wide to join in Macclesfield's prosperity. Outworkers thrived too - houses were built with stairs leading up from the outside and garrets to house the looms, the weavers and their families. Many can still be seen in Macclesfield -- the most prominent being in Paradise Street. The Macclesfield weavers at this time were an affluent lot, and wages were high.

However, when the Napoleonic Wars ended in 1815 the silk industry's fortunes took a tumble. Many manufacturers went bankrupt and many of the workers found themselves without a job, and, thanks to the war, prices had risen sharply. There was great deal of poverty.

This depression was followed, in the early 1820s, by a period of booming trade. More mills for silk throwing were built and it is estimated that over 10,000 people were employed in the industry -- many coming from out of town. There were 70 factories and 5,000 looms.

But another depression was on the way. Before 1824, the silk manufacturers had been blessed with heavy duties on foreign silk. An Act of Parliament in 1824 reduced these duties and there were more reductions over the next two years. As if this was not enough, the duty on raw silk was reduced and so, in 1826, all the silk in town was sent to Charles Roe's original mill in Park Green for tax refund estimates. From then on it became known as the Depot Mill.

The rise and fall of fortunes in the silk trade continued throughout the 19th century and, in the latter part of the century, the workers had to face another problem as well -- that of seasonal trade. Because of the fashion fads and fancies of the time, there were times of the year when workers went on short time and they were sometimes without work completely. Distressed workers were often put to work constructing new roads in the borough. During the building of Macclesfield Infirmary, silk workers were the "navvies". Another road built at the time was Westminster Road, named in honour of the Marquis of Westminster who had interested himself in the Infirmary.

Victoria Road, then called Bowfield Lane, was widened in 1865 and as the condition of so many weavers was so bad that large numbers of unemployed were found work in the construction of that road, also. For this purpose, and the construction of Cumberland Street and Westminster Road, £15,000 was borrowed by the Corporation under the terms of an Act of Parliament entitled "An Act to authorise the advance of money out of the Consolidated Fund to a limited amount for the carrying on of Public Works and the Employment of the Poor".

The Maxfilt Weavers

A leaflet was freely distributed in Macclesfield during the latter half of the 19th century, designed to warn silk weavers of the "folly" of strikes and also of the folly of the demon drink.

It was written in the dialect of "Maxfilt" and is thought to have been composed by a mill owner - some say Mr William Brocklehurst, M.P.

Vote for Brocklehurst ... electioneering at the Brocklehurst Mill, Hurdsfield, in 1906 when Colonel W. B. Brocklehurst was elected.

Prestbury - lane referred to in the verse is the workhouse.

A Few Words to the Maxfilt Weaver

Aye lad, thou'rt a weaver I see sure enuff,
I con tell by th' mak of thy coat an' its stuff;
An owd velvet powcher, aw shinin' wi' grease,
An th' billy-cock top of thy yed's of a piece.
Aw reckon thee'st "fastened" thy best bits o' duds,
An' thy shirt has na' bin for a fortnight i'th' suds;
Thee look'st welly clemmed - why what's up wi' the mon-
Ah, thee winna say owt, but aw'll tell if aw con.
May happen thee'st playing thee now for a cane,
Or may be its shute that thou'st wanting again;
Thee'st bin waiting aw morning for work i'the camp,
And just now thee'st thinking of taking a tramp.
"Aw winna be humbugged a thisans" you say;
"Aw'll start off to Lankesheer this very day;
"For work's up to nothi' in Macclesfield nai;
"Aw'll have it i' Manchester, mon, or aw'll try."
Well, lad! aw just wait a bit - conna thee see,
As how a deal cheaper an gainer 'twould be,
To get it a'whoam - for th' clogs'll be war,
An' thy brass aw the leiter, by tramping so far.
Hai leets it that garrets are empty i'th taan,
While weavers have jobs i'th' country aw raand;
Thow may tak' my word for it, there's summit amiss,
And some folk are wrung, or we should na see this.
There's mesters, I know, are no friends to th' poor,
And money o'er-lookers are tyrants I'm sure;
But reet well thee knowst, George, I need not tell you,
There's mony a weaver is naw but a foo'.
When a mester's i' Lunnun his orders he gets,
He comes down to Maxfilt, an' price list he sets;

The canes are aw gaited, the weavers agree,
Till some chap 'gins grumble - "this work's very dree."
Then a Delegate goes to the "Swan" and belike
He sits up i'th' club room and orders a strike;
Then th' Union turns out, and the shuttles drop down,
And hundreds o' weavers are walkin' the town.
Then the publican's busy, aye, aw the week throo,
And there's cursin', and swearin', and drinkin' enoo,
Till Saturday neet, but they are na content;
An' I needn't tell thee, mon, how Sunday is spent.
Then o' Monday we see the poor women about,
An' blankets and sheets are aw sent up the spout.
For the children can't clem, tho' they work at the mill,
That th' drunken owd fayther his liquor may swill.
Then says mester to manager, "This is no fun;
The orders are given, the work must be done;
So send it to Ormskirk - wherever you please,
For I'm bless'd if I put up with weavers like these."
The weaver wauks out, and the weaver comes in;
His elbows get ragged - his cheeks they grow thin,
An' well he mit say, "I'll be ta'en for a ghost,"
For he conna stond streight 'bout he leans 'gen a poast.
Then to Prestbury-lane, when the winter sets,
He creeps; but, says Froggatt, it's nowt but "go in",
When th' soup kitchen's opened, an' to ti he goes,
Wi' a can i' his hond, an' a drop at his nose.
Ah, mon, thou'rt a foo', an' just tauk as thee may,
Thou'rt drivin' the silk weaving business away -
An' I fear me that Maxfilt will always be poor,
Till its poverty knockers are never heard more.

3 "Royal" Macclesfield

By Royal Charter

The Royal Charter referred to the Merchants' guild of Macclesfield. A Guild was a brotherhood of the merchants or traders in the town whereby the trade of the town became vested in their hands. They had powers to restrict people not admitted to their association from selling in the town apart from at fair time.

It is probable that, about this time, the ancient Guild hall was erected in the Market Place and it was there that the members held their meetings and transacted their business. It has been described as a "quaint old structure" with a double flight of stone steps surmounted by iron railings which led to the main entrance. The hall was demolished in 1823 to make way for the more modern Town Hall which was enlarged and improved in 1869. The various guilds each had their own coats of arms, and a number of taverns in the town and surrounding area were named after these. The

Old Town Hall.

29

The area now known as Mill Lane and Mill Green used to lead to the old fulling mill on the "Pool of Macclesfield". This is how Pool Street got its name. Here is pictured some members of the Bullock family of Rock House, Sutton, shopping in Mill Lane in the early part of this century.

Blacksmiths Arms at Henbury still exists and there were also the Moulders Arms, the Joiners Arms and the Gardeners Arms.

In the Charter, the burgess are described as being free from passage, pontage and stallage throughout the County of Chester. "Passage" meant money paid as a "toll" over rivers and streams and "pontage" the same for a ferry or for bridge. "Stallage" was money charged for permission to erect stalls or booths in any market town.

The Prince and the Mill

The Prince's Mill (later known as the king's Mill) was thought for a long while to have been around Mill Green. The names Old Mill Green, Mill Lane and an old tavern in that vicinity called the Millstone gave rise to this conjecture. In fact, the Royal Mill was on the River Bollin near the bottom of Brunswick Steps. The other mill was a fulling mill on the "Pool of Macclesfield" (hence Pool Street). This is probably the first textile mill in

Macclesfield but was for fulling - a process which thickens and stretches wool, not for silk weaving, for which Macclesfield was later renowned.

Undoubtedly the wool came from the Macclesfield Forest area and from Monks Heath and the Abbey near Leek. These Mill Green premises are recorded in an indenture dated 1356 between Robert Le Walker and Edward, Prince of Wales.

The road which led to the royal mill at the time of the charter is now called Hibel Road.

The Royal Bakehouse or Kings Oven was situated near the old Guild Hall in Churchside where the former police station used to be at the side of the present Town Hall. The property remained in the possession of the Crown until 1808 when it was sold and purchased by Timothy Jones who converted it into a wine and spirit cellars, the entrance to which was known in the early part of the 19th century as the Long Entry.

In 1270 Prince Edward set out for Palestine to take part in the Crusade against the Turks or Saracens, accompanied by nearly 200 English nobles and gentry. It is highly probable that a number of local gentry and their servants accompanied the Prince, as Earl of Chester. Doubtless these included the Leghs of Adlington and High Legh, the Worths of Tytherington, Sir John Baskervyle of Withington, the Davenports of Henbury, Marton and Capesthorne and the Thorneycrofts of Thornecroft. Before he left, the Prince made Eleanor the Lady of the Manor of Macclesfield.

Macclesfield Castle

Nothing now remains of Macclesfield, Castle, a castellated structure that stood a very short distance from the Parish Church at the top of Backwallgate, which was formerly called Souter Lane.

The last remains of this once fine building were removed in the 1930s, taken to the Corporation yard and, it is believed, used as foundation stone for a number of roads.

Often described as the Castle of the Duke of Buckingham, enough had survived the centuries to show that the feudal mansion built at the end of the fourteenth century was a fortified mansion and citadel of no mean proportion.

The Castle was built by John de Legh about the year 1400. He was the son of Robert de Legh of Adlington and he took up residence within our borough - from which fact he became known as John de Macclesfield. A glance at the list of Mayors shows that in the years 1358-9, the wearer of the civic robes and occupant of the mayoral chair was John de Macclesfield. John was an official at the court of Richard II and a clerk in holy orders, although he had five sons by Katherine Kingesley who lived near to the Castle. He was a substantial land and property owner in the area.

An artist's impression of the remains of Macclesfield Castle as they were in the 1920s. The drawing is taken from the front cover of a leaflet sold by J. Halstead Cutts, ironmonger, 32 Mill Street.

In 1398, John petitioned Richard II for a licence to "embattle and kernellite with stone and lime the buildings recently begun in his house or mansion in the town of Maxfelde and that he may hold same to himself and to his heirs for ever. And that he may have a grant of six oaks from the forest of Maxfelde for the same building"

On the 30th August, 1398, the king issued Letters Patent acceding to the request. A stone bearing the date 1400 is built into the walls of a passage called "Palace Yard" which led from Mill Street to the building and this probably refers to the date when Macclesfield's Castle was completed . This was formerly called Godyaf Lane.

An old writer describes it as "A massive stone building, the central portion of which was square in form, with two wings and five turrets or towers - a central turret, and one at each angle. It was very extensive and capable of accommodating a considerable number of men at arms and retainers. The Castle was surrounded by a strong wall which enclosed a spacious courtyard and had stables, kennels and outhouses in the vicinity."

Keys at the Castle Inn, Backwallgate, are thought to be from the castellated manor house of the Duke of Buckingham.
This photograph of those leisurely and sunny days in the 1930s that seemed to go on for ever shows the pub used to sell Adshead Ales.

John de Legh's son, also called John de Macclesfield disposed of his estates in Macclesfield and Bosley to Humphrey Stafford, Duke of Buckingham, in the early part of the 15th century, it went into the possession of the Stanleys, Earls of Derby.

An old scribe by the name of Webb, who wrote *A History of Vale Royal* in 1624 describes it : "In Macclesfield are yet to be seen some ruins of the ancient manor house of the renowned Humphrey, Duke of Buckingham, who, as report goeth, kept here is princely residence about the time of King Edward the fourth, and of whose great hospitality then, much tradition is reported."

The brave Humphrey, Duke of Buckingham, was slain in the war of the Roses on the 10th of July, 1459. His son, Henry Stafford, Duke of Buckingham, was beheaded in the Market Place at Salisbury on November 2nd, 1483, by order of Richard III. This is how the Earl of Derby came to be owner .

Parts of the masonry, including massive buttresses which formed part of this historic building, may be seen in Back Wallgate and Palace Yard.

33

The Longbowmen of Macclesfield

Was it the close vicinity of Macclesfield Forest that enabled men of Macclesfield to be so adept with the longbow? Such was the skill the men of these parts acquired with the bow and arrow, now associated with Robin and Will Scarlett, that the Black Prince would only use the men of Cheshire during his wars.

Victoria Road, where the new District General and Macclesfield Cricket Club now both stand was formerly known as Bowfield Lane or Boughey Lane. Before these buildings and the houses that now occupy the road were built, it was a "narrow dark and paved path" which led to a farm. Historian John Earls discovered that this was where the Macclesfield bowmen practised archery - in a large field in the vicinity , and there attained that skill for which they were famous.

Francis Duckworth, in his "History of Cheshire" says the bowmen of Macclesfield were on the scene long before the "Bowmen of Cheshire" became famous in their own right. He says : "It will be remembered that in Edward 1st's Welsh wars, crossbowmen were combined with the Macclesfield archers, but 50 years later the Cheshire men had quite mastered the art of shooting with the long bow and its slow and cumbrous predecessor (the crossbow) had disappeared."

This leads to some interesting speculation. Was the charter granted to Macclesfield by Edward 1st because of the Macclesfield bowmen who helped him in his Welsh wars? There is no documentary evidence of this. It can only be supposition. Further, when Edward 1st went on his Crusade, was he accompanied by archers from Macclesfield? Macclesfield's archers accompanied Sir Perkin Legh of Lyme and the Black Prince in the French Wars. In 1346, the Battle of Crecy resulted in the overthrow of the French army thanks to the tactics of the archers. For his services in the war, Sir Perkin Legh was rewarded with the gift of Lyme Park. Later, Sir Piers and, presumably, the Macclesfield bowmen, were at the Battle of Agincourt with Henry V.

Sir John Savage took a number of Cheshire bowmen with him to Bosworth in 1485 and Christopher Savage, Mayor of Macclesfield (who was killed at Flodden Field in 1513) was accompanied by a number of burgesses of the town. So many Macclesfield men were slain at this battle that it was necessary to petition the king for the means to create fresh burgesses in order that the affairs of the Borough could be carried out.

During the Black Prince's time, it was recorded that the archers were quite a rabble! They were certainly not well disciplined but, because of their rowdy ways before battle, and their threats to go into the employment of "other company" their lands and goods were forfeited until after the battle.

One famous quotation says of these men, "Raised from the lowest occupation, they lorded it over their superiors and their insolence and arrogance knew no bounds."

The Black Prince and the Black Death

The Black Prince visited Macclesfield on a number of occasions and , it must be presumed, his main purposes were both for the recruitment of archers and for a hunting trip in both the Forest and the royal parklands. In 1353, he stayed at the manor house which had to be repaired before his arrival.

He also visited this area in 1349 shortly after the Black Death had claimed over one third of the population . There was poverty and distress and considerable disorder. Whether he came to put the place in order again after the Plague or to recruit for the French Wars is a matter of conjecture. Perhaps he was killing two birds with one stone.

For one hundred years or so after his death, the anniversary of his passing was commemorated in Macclesfield.

During the Civil War

During the reign of Charles 1st, Macclesfield was not represented in Parliament. When Oliver Cromwell chopped off the King's head, Macclesfield appears to have been in more or less complete agreement, being on the side of the Parliament forces.

On two occasions, Royalists tried to capture the town. Sir Thomas Aston took Macclesfield in 1642 and there is no record of any resistance being made by the townsfolk. A few months later, the Roundheads, under Sir William Brereton, captured it back. Colonel Legh of Adlington Hall (whose ancestors still live in that stately house) was a Royalist and he brought his men down to the road to Macclesfield in an attempt to kick the Parliamentarians out, but he was not successful. The Parliamentarians were commanded by Colonel Mainwaring who, after securing Macclesfield, promptly attacked Adlington Hall, where there was a good arsenal. A siege lasted for some 14 days before the Royalist Leghs surrendered and the area around Macclesfield remained strongly Pro-Parliament for the remainder of the Civil War until the monarchy was restored in 1660.

It was at this time that the steward of Macclesfield Forest, James Stanley, the seventh Earl of Derby, lost his head. He was a Royalist and the stewardship and any money arising from the post passed to Sir William Brereton of Handforth as a reward for his Parliamentary support.

This era saw the virtual end of Macclesfield Forest as a hunting ground for royalty. Over the years, settlers had built homesteads on the bleak ground and more and more farmed the land when Sir William, Obviously with his eye on his purse, began to rent out parts of the Forest for grazing.

The Bate Hall Hotel, Chestergate, as it was in the sixteenth century.

4 A Healthy Society?

The Gutters

The Plague hit Macclesfield again, in common with most other parts of England, in the year 1603. it is on record that the mortality was particularly high in the part of the town called "The Gutters" where there were a large number of very squalid houses and shops and public houses. Before gas was introduced to Macclesfield, the town had a number of tallow makers because most of the townsfolk who could afford it used candles for light. The majority of tallow chandlers were concentrated around the Gutters.

A rainy day in the Market Place in the 1950s before the market stalls were removed.

Next page

The ancient market tradition lived on in the Market Place until the 1960s when, in the name of progress, the stalls went.

Old charabancs line up at the side of a smoke-stained Town Hall in the 1930s.

Many of the stalls in front of the Town Hall and along by the Unicorn and Union gateways were open-air ones, exposed to the worst of Macclesfield weather. In this interesting picture, taken during the last years of the reign of Queen Victoria, the Bulls head Hotel can be seen in the background. What this delightful shot also shows is, in the right foreground, a cat that is just about to steal from a barrel of oysters!
Oysters were brought in to Macclesfield on most market days and were a cheap food in those times. Whether they were fresh or not is another matter, although there was the advantage of a regular train service delivery.

For many years, stalls were erected outside the Town Hall, in the area of Macclesfield rightly called the Market Place. Now they are all removed. In addition to the stalls, local farmers would sell their wares from baskets that were placed around the perimeter of the Market Place. Here, outside the former District Bank, can be seen one such trader. These baskets extended down Brunswick Street to where the modern police station now stands.

The Gutters was situated behind the old church and went as far as Goose Lane, which is now called Brunswick Street. The area round here had a bad reputation and this was reflected in its name, which was something of a derisory one.

Perhaps due to the overcrowding in the area, and certainly because of the poor, if not non-existent sanitation, the Plague struck particularly virulently in this area.

Today, there can be seen on the Cophurst Edge, near to the Hanging Gate public house a stone which is known as the "Plague Stone" which has a cross carved on either side. It is said country folk brought their produce to this stone and buying and selling was carried on near to it. No doubt the coins were washed in vinegar before changing hands.

A market was held three quarters of a mile out of Macclesfield, according to a document preserved at Capesthorne Hall, and Macclesfield's magistrates compiled a weekly list of how many people were affected by the plague. A watch was kept to keep all Macclesfield people in the town. In the month from September 3rd to October 3rd, there are 70 deaths recorded in the Burials Register and, from these records, it is known that the plague was particularly active in the Gutters, Dog Lane (later Stanley Street and now where the Grosvenor Precinct is) and Back Street (King Edward Street).

Previous page

To the left of the Town Hall, the Union Gateway (and an Elizabethan leaded light window). In the shop window are acetylene lamps - think how the meat would pick up the smell of the oil. At the side of the Town Hall the framework of the shop could still be seen in 1988, against the municipal buildings wall.

The Shambles

Also in the Gutters was a large covered space devoted to butchers' stalls, known as the shambles. Over the centuries, butchers were prevented from having their shops in the streets of the town; adjacent to their stalls were the fishmongers' stalls.

Most of the fishmongers gathered together on the pavement in front of the Sun Inn in Chestergate. This was later pulled down to make way for Parr's Bank and now the site is occupied by the National Westminster Bank.

Butter and cheese were sold by the Guild Hall. This site became occupied by nothing more worthy than a car park. Market day for the Shambles was a Monday but it was altered to Tuesdays, in line with all other goods sold at Macclesfield's markets in 1815. Prior to this the meat was slaughtered on a Sunday and this offended many people.

As time moved on, the meat sellers were unhappy about having to congregate in the one spot and wanted to open shops in other parts of the town; but, the local authorities resisted their demands and there was much controversy.

Many butchers, and some fishmongers, started to erect stalls outside their own homes to sell their meat and fish and one butcher, presumably as a "test case" was taken to High Court - the corporation of Macclesfield won the day. This was in 1843 but, because of the national move towards free trade, the corporation eventually allowed meat and fish to be sold in other parts of the town.

The Shambles Market and site was purchased by Macclesfield Council in 1900 with the intention of building a new covered market, but this never came to fruition and, just before the outbreak of the second world war, the site was levelled.

The approach to the Shambles from the Market Place was through two covered passageways to the left of the Town Hall, both of which have been demolished. There are now market stalls and a car park (not to mention a public toilet) where these entrances - the Union and Unicorn Gateways - used to stand. Within a radius of only a few yards, there were five taverns - the Roebuck, Punch Bowl, Market Vaults, Borough Arms and Unicorn. Further on was "The Feathers" which, during the early and middle parts of this century developed rather an unsavoury reputation. I shall say no more.

When the new Town hall was built on the site of the Guild Hall in 1823, part of the new building was used as the Butter Market. Farmers and their families sold eggs, vegetables, poultry, cheese and fruit; once a month, the premises were used as a wholesale market for cheese - Cheshire cheese made in and around Macclesfield.

The last trader in the butter market ceased in 1939 and, for most of the time since then, it has been used for storing the outdoor market stalls when they are not in use.

5 Law and Order

Barbaric Tortures

Macclesfield appears to have been a town that required to be ruled by an iron hand - if not an iron bridle! in the times of the Tudors and Stuarts.

In 1662, among other articles delivered into the possession of the sergeant at mace was a "bridle for a curst queane" that is, a punishment for what was also termed a "passionate and brawling woman". This Scolds bridle is still preserved in the museum, and it would appear that the burgesses of olden times must have found it difficult to restrain the tempers and tongues of their womenfolk. Perhaps another viewpoint is that the poor unfortunate ladies were dominated by cruel and thoughtless menfolk. I am happy to let you choose!

The cucking stool, sometimes known as a tumbril or trebuchet. Cuckstoolpit Hill derived its name from this custom.

To curb a scold's tongue
Put a brank on her head -
It will make her as silent
As though she were dead.

Macclesfield was not alone in having a brank or bridle for punishment, but few of these barbarous devices remain.

This Bridle, a cage that was placed over the unfortunate woman's head, had a piece of iron which was forced into the mouth over the tongue. She would be then led about the streets.

In addition to this item of torture, there was a peculiar form of straight jacket, also made of iron, known as the Brank. It consisted of four tiers of iron, about the thickness of a man's finger, fitted with joints and hung together with chains. On each side were cuffs to secure the hands which would, effectually, defy all attempts to escape. Anyone accused of wrong doing in those days, whether man or woman, would well have trembled. The unlucky people "branked" were led to the jail in this device.

There was yet another method of punishing offending women - a form of device which had its origins in the darker ages when unfortunate practisers of natural arts were often accused of being witches or under the influence of the devil. This was the Ducking or Cucking Stool - from whence the name Cuckstoolpit Hill was derived. This is an area behind the Central Station, where there used to be an old and narrow wooden bridge over which pedestrians had to pass to get to the Hill. This steep lane connected the Waters with Macclesfield Common and, at the bottom of the hill, was the deepest pool of water, or pit, on the River Bollin. Here, there was a stool or chair fixed at the end of a long pole and in this seat, unfortunate females were placed and soused three times as a punishment for various offences.

There seems to be little record of what the "offences" were. Witchcraft was one and the superstitious townsfolk would (as their country counterparts would, also) blame any misfortune from illness to a bad harvest or freak weather conditions on any person who they distrusted and were frightened of. Elderly ladies, often because of knowledge acquired over the years, were used as cheap doctors, midwives and chemists and it was often these people who were blamed for catastrophes.

Guardians of the Law

The Borough Police Force was inaugurated on the 19th January, 1836 and William Lockett was appointed the first Chief Constable. The Watch Committee decided that he should have six efficient Constables, four for the day and two for the night, the day constables to take it in turns to be on duty with the night police. Also, there should be four special constables for Saturday nights and Sundays.

Their uniform included tall hats, the crown of the hat being covered with patent leather with a narrow strip of the same material down either side. They had double breasted swallow tail coats and white trousers.

The official history of the Macclesfield Borough Police Force gives a few instances of punishments in those times. On January 22nd, 1843 a 19 year old youth convicted of burglary was transported for 10 years. Eight days later, a 17 year old youth on suspicion of breaking into a slaughterhouse and stealing 50lbs of pork was transported for seven years. On July 9th, a man (43) was fined five shillings and set in the stocks for being drunk and disorderly and two boys, each aged 11, accused of stealing a rabbit were each given 14 days in the clink and were ordered to be whipped on the seventh day.

There are frequent entries in the charge books of the stocks which were, for many years, on display in West Park but they went for salvage during the second world war.

Isaac Finney's *"Macclesfelde in ye Olden Time"* says "In many places the stocks were often constructed as to serve as both stocks and whipping posts, the post which supported the stocks being made sufficiently high, were furnished near the top with iron clasps to fasten round the wrists of offenders, and hold them securely during the infliction of punishment. The stocks formerly used at Macclesfield were not so constructed; when a case of whipping or flogging occurred, use was made of the top of the steps leading into the old Town Hall (the Guild Hall) where the culprit (male or female, for both sexes were whipped) was secured to the railing prior to the infliction of punishment. The iron rails served both for this purpose and also for hanging, as in the case of the deserter who was hanged from them when the Duke of Cumberland passed through the town in 1745 in pursuit of Prince Charles Edward Stuart."

"The last case of whipping in Macclesfield occurred about the year 1831 when a young man was publicly whipped in front of the Town Hall."

"In alluding to the old stocks we may well remark after their demolition in the year 1828, new ones were made of iron and placed under the balcony of the new Town Hall and were occasionally used; but after a short time they were also dispensed with and put by as lumber so put by as lumber so that now the pounishment is altogether abolished".

The Mayor's Accounts , with respect of the use of the stocks,
pillory and bridle show:

	s.	d.
1708-9 Spent about whipping a woman at the Rogues Post		6
Spent about bridling a woman	1	0
1709-10 Spent about whipping some lads	1	0
1711-12 Spent about putting a madman in Gaol		4
Spent about bridling a woman		6
Spent about setting a man in the stocks		6
More at whipping another man	1	4

At putting another man in Gaol	1	4
Spent at bridling a scolding woman		6
1737-38 Paid John Burgess for making Cuckstool	10	0
1756-7 Paid Mr Huley for timber for Stock & Pillory	18	10
1757-8 Paid for lock and key for the Stocks		9

1794 Property of Mayor's inter alia - 2 Bridles for Scolds:
one in the Town Hall and one in the Workhouse and the
Workhouse and a portable Pillory.

The Mayor of Macclesfield in 1830, Dr W.B. Dickenson, is recorded as having said that the bridle was applied to its barbarous purpose during his term of office and this was, it is thought, the last time it was used.

The Market Cross, or part of it, has now been returned to almost its original setting and stands in front of the Parish church. It was formerly in the Market Place and is probably an old preaching station or, possibly, a mark to denote a meeting place for trade - a "mark-et". From its base, proclamations were read. The Cross was taken down in 1795 when improvements were being made and, somehow it got into the possession of Matthew William Whitney, a farmer, who re-erected it in a field at Upton over the grave of a pet dog. There it remained until it was removed to West Park in 1858 - but not before a piece of the upright shaft had been used by the farmer as a roller. The letter "M.W.W.1798" can still be seen on the part of the cross remaining.

The man responsible for much of Macclesfield's demise was William Huskisson, the President of the Board of Trade, who reduced duties on foreign silks in 1826.

By way of retribution, he met his death during the opening ceremony of George Stephenson's Liverpool to Manchester Railway on September 30th, 1830. He was run over by an engine.

From this time, old methods of transport were changing rapidly and railway lines sprouted across the country. In August, 1831, a new line was opened from Manchester to London but this did not pass through Macclesfield, and those who wished to use it had to travel to Crewe. The following are the chief horse-drawn coaches which plied between Macclesfield and other centres in 1830:

Macclesfield Arms
from the Macclesfield Arms Hotel, Jordangate
To London: "The Royal Mail" every morning at 11-30 through Leek, Ashbourne, Derby, Leicester and Northampton.
To Manchester: "The London Royal Mail" every afternoon at 2 o'clock.
To London: "The Defiance" every morning at 8 o'clock, performs the same service as the "Royal Mail"

Angel & Bull's Head
from the Angel Hotel and the Bull's Head:
To London: "The Royal Telegraph" every evening at 6 o'clock through Leek, Ashbourne, etc., to Fetter Lane, London.
To Manchester: "The Mercury" every afternoon at 2 o'clock.
To Birmingham: "The Royal Express" every morning at 10 o'clock through Leek, Cheadle, Uttoxeter and Lichfield, to the "Hen and Chickens", Birmingham.
To Manchester: "The Rover" every evening at a quarter before five.
To Newcastle-under-Lyme: "The Jolly Potter" every day (Sundays excepted) at a quarter past five in the afternoon through Congleton, Red Bull, Barslow, Hanley, to the Hotel, Newcastle.
To Congleton: "The Comet" every Sunday, Tuesday, Thursday and Saturday evenings at 7 o'clock.

Other Coaching Houses
Other coaching houses in Macclesfield were the Pack Horse, Jordangate and Hibberts General Coaching Office, the Flying Horse, Chestergate from which yards were coaches to London, Birmingham, Manchester, Buxton, Liverpool and Chester.

6 Transport

The Canal

The Macclesfield Canal was finally opened for traffic on November 10th, 1831, and it was a big day for the town. This waterway connects the Trent and Mersey Canal near Black Bull in Staffordshire with the Peak Forest Canal near Marple. Two processions of boats passed along the canal for its opening, the one from the north consisting of 52 barges and the one from the south, 25. Several were occupied by committee and directors of the canal company and the remaining boats contained coal, salt, lime and stone which were the chief products of the locality it was hoped would be carried. Afterwards, there was a procession to the Town Hall preceded by the Macclesfield Cavalry.

It is thought that the famous engineer James Brindley designed the aqueduct in Byrons Lane, Sutton, although it was not built until after his death. As a boy, Brindley served as an apprentice to a millwright named Bennett who conducted his business in Gurnet, Sutton.

The Railway

The first railway to be constructed in Macclesfield was in 1845 - the Macclesfield Branch of the Manchester and Birmingham. The station was near Beech Lane Bridge. As with the opening of the canal, this was a great event which was followed by a huge banquet, but not before the Mayor and civic worthies had been taken to Manchester and back.

The North Staffordshire Railway Company - later to be nicknamed "The Knotty" after its emblem the Staffordshire knot - began to cut a line to join Macclesfield with London. It reached Congleton in 1848 and for that year until it reached Macclesfield a coach service was run from Macclesfield to Congleton . This line came through the centre of Macclesfield to a station at Hibel Road. It was not until 1872 that a third railway came to town. This was a branch of the Sheffield and Lincoln Railway and ran from Marple to Macclesfield, where it joined the North Staffordshire Railway. The Central Station was opened in 1873.

Hibel Road, where the second station was built, was once a dark, narrow and badly paved street leading from Jordangate to the Waters and Hurdsfield. It was know as Cockshute Lane in its early days - the "sport" of cockfighting being carried on around there.

The construction of the new Macclesfield railways necessitated the destruction of many landmarks. In the middle of the Waters there stood a tavern called the Cross Keys and this was demolished in 1872 when the Waters Green Railway Station (the present Central Station) was built. The Cross Keys was the emblem of Thomas Savage, Archbishop of York, and, despite it ecclesiastic connections, was the scene of much dissipation.

The Flying Horse Hotel, (pictured left) now demolished, in Chestergate. This was one of the several coaching hostelries - hence its name - and served passengers to and from Chester.

Hibel Road station bedecked with glorious flowers in 1948 awaiting the arrival of the Princess Elizabeth for an official visit.

Colonel W. B. Brocklehust, M.P. for the Macclesfield Division, elected January 18th, 1906 with a majority of 494.

7 Elections to Parliament

Despite having a population of over 30,000 in 1830, the town had no Member of Parliament. There was much agitation for redistribution of Parliamentary seats and there are records of riots and disturbances at meetings which had to be dispersed by the cavalry. The Whig inhabitants of Macclesfield produced a petition to the Crown, signed by 4,200 Macclesfield men. In 1818, Macclesfield supported a mass meeting at Saint Peter's Field, Manchester, which to go down in history as the Peterloo Massacre. The demand for reform continued to grow and the Reform Act was eventually passed in 1832. Macclesfield was then able to send two Members of Parliament to the Commons. There was an election contested by three people and the result was: John Ryle 464 votes; John Brocklehurst 424 and Thomas Grimsditch 341. It was not until 1867 that the second Reform Act extended the right to vote to all ratepayers and to lodgers paying an annual rent of 10 s. (50 pence) or more. In 1884, the boundary was changed and Macclesfield then could only return one Member.

There was much bribery and corruption at elections throughout the country and the Parliamentary Elections and Corrupt Practices Act was passed in 1879 to facilitate the imprisonment of those who influenced voters. But it did not stop corrupt practice in Macclesfield and, in the 1880 Macclesfield election, when W.C.Brocklehurst and D. Chadwick were elected, a petition was lodged in the High Court by four Macclesfield voters and the election was declared void. A Royal Commission was appointed which met 53 times and it was concluded that the elections of 1865, 1868, 1874 and 1880 had witnessed massive bribery. The election agents were imprisoned.

One of the Members of Parliament who was convicted of corruption was David Chadwick. This photograph shows him and supporters on the hustings outside the Town Hall during the election of 1865.

8 Colourful Characters

Macclesfield is a unique town with a unique history. It's had its fair share of colourful characters over the years as well - characters either adopted, bred or nurtured.

Here we take a look at a mere handful of the many.

There's the man who abducted an heiress and who prompted Charles Dickens to write Oliver Twist; there's the Macclesfield Aborigine who also played a great role in Australia's history; there's the man who walked backwards and there's the Canadian Collosus who made Treacle Town his home.

All larger than life fold with larger than life tales.

The Moonman of Macclesfield

The Moonman of Macclesfield.

In the early part of the year 1835, the reports of the fertility of the land in the neighbourhood of Port Philip, Australia, led to an expedition from Van Diemen's Land (Tasmania) with the object of exploring the district.

The leader was John Bateman, the Governor of Tasmania, and the party landed at Geelong on May 26th, 1835.

The new arrivals were amazed to find a gigantic white man who had lived among the aborigines for over 30 years and who adopted all the habits and customs of the natives.

This white man was William Buckley, born at Marton near Macclesfield, who came to the thriving industrial town of Macclesfield as a youth to find work and became a bricklayer. He was later sentenced to transportation for life.

Buckley was nicknamed Methody Bill because he and his family followed the preachings of John Wesley - no stranger to Macclesfield. While in Macclesfield he met up with some local ruffians and they plotted to rob a coach that had been visiting Henbury Hall and was returning to Chester. Their plot was discovered and armed militia thwarted their attempt. Buckley fled and joined the King's Own Regiment. He fought the French in Holland and, after being wounded, was sent back to England, where he again fell in with a "bad lot". He was found in possession of some stolen cloth and sentenced to transportation to the penal colony now known as Australia.

Buckley was one of a large number of convicts who were placed in the transport ship "Calcutta" and in the month of April the vessel set sail. In charge of the convicts was Colonel Collins who was entrusted with the duty of establishing a penal settlement at Port Philip in what in now Victoria.

On arrival in Australia the occupants of the ship landed and set up camp. Buckley and twelve others escaped and roamed the barren land for a week without food. His companion, desperate for food, went back to the camp but Buckley appears to have liked his freedom better than food and stayed on his own. Two of the convicts who said they were returning to camp were never heard of again.

Buckley was no doubt afraid of the punishment that would be handed out of him if he was to return but he was totally ignorant of the vast and inhospitable land in which he found himself. He walked on alone and reached a river where he hid from a tribe of native aboriginals, finding a few berries and vegetation which he ate.

Eventually, he made the decision to return to the convict camp and set off, picking up a wooden stick that was sticking out of the ground

When the aborigines saw him, he was the first white man they had come across and he towered head and shoulders above them. He was also holding the spear that had belonged to their chief, Murrangurk, who had recently died. The moon was full and, to the primitive people who set eyes on him, he was a Moon God -a reincarnation of their chief.

Methody Bill, the Macclesfield bricklayer, was fed on toasted witchety grubs, kangaroo, wallaby and birds' eggs and wrapped in the warm skins of possums. He was taught the ways of the tribe as a newborn babe would be taught, for he was re-born. He later recalled how he despaired of ever seeing a white man again and lost all track of time. He adopted the aborigines' language and had almost forgotten the use of his own native tongue when he was discovered some 30 years later by the Governor of Tasmania and his party.

Buckley, who was thoroughly conversant with the dialect of the natives, acted as an interpreter to the British pioneers. Not only was he the means of preventing the exploration party from being murdered but he was able to promote a friendship between the members of Bateman's expedition and the aborigines. He was successful in arranging for the purchase of a large tract of land on which the great city of Melbourne was built.

Governor Bateman granted a free pardon to the Moon Man in consideration of the fact that his services as an interpreter and mediator had been invaluable.

Buckley remained in the neighbourhood of Port Philip for two years and witnessed the foundation of Melbourne and , when the Governor's house was erected on Bateman Hill, he superintended much of the work - a task he was well able to do as he had been a bricklayer. In the neighbourhood of Melbourne, there is a cascade of water known as Buckley Falls and a common phrase in the Australia tongue is "not stand a Buckley's", meaning to stand very little chance indeed.

He afterwards went to Tasmania and spent the remainder of his life at Hobart Town. Up to the time of his death (he was run over by a horse and carriage) he received a Government pension of £100 a year and continued to act as an interpreter between the British and the aborigines.

Backwards to Buxton

In the year 1875, a Macclesfield publican had a bet. This rather unusual wager was that he could walk, backwards, from Macclesfield to Buxton across some of the most rugged countryside in England within three hours.

He did it.

But what is more remarkable is that 27 years later, when this person was aged 62, he did it again.

This extraordinary pedestrian was Mr John Alcock, the landlord of the Oxford Road Tavern, an all-round sportsman and athlete, who first accomplished this astonishing feat in September, 1875.

It appears that Mr Alcock's athletic prowess had been called in to question by some of his customers and associates. Mr Alcock was a very proud man and no doubt he was the subject of some "ribbing". The result was that he hit on the idea of not only walking to Macclesfield - a steep and gruelling walk- within three hours but performing this backwards.

It is hardly suprising there were plenty of people willing to bet against him, and John Alcock put down £20 of his own money. This stunt was on the cards for a few weeks before it took place and it is recorded that betting circles showed interest from the nearby Potteries and from Manchester and Stockport.

On the Wednesday morning, a crowd of several hundred had gathered in the Market Place by 6.30, ready for the off at seven. A condition of the bet was that Alcock should have his face pointed towards Macclesfield at all times, not being allowed to even slightly turn his head in the direction in which he was going. Punctually at seven o'clock, by the Old Church, Alcock started on his journey from the Church gates, reversing the usual walking order of heel and toe to toe and heel. In front, or rather at the back, of him was a "pioneer" who cleared the way while facing him was a "rear guard" who acted as helmsman or guide.

The first mile, which seemed the most difficult to Alcock, was accomplished in 12 and a half minutes and after this he seemed to get into better spirits and went along at a rattling pace, keeping the hundreds of people who accompanied him part of the distance on a semi trot. He passed Walker Barn (three miles on) at twenty minutes to eight and accomplished his forth mile in under the hour. Past the Cat and Fiddle, where there were fifty people cheering him on, he was asked to rest awhile but he said there was no need to be concerned and challenged the "losers" to walk the same way back again.

He arrived in Buxton with 15 minutes in hand and, besides the many coins of the realm that came his way, his backers presented him with a silver cup in commemoration of the extraordinary event.

It was some 27 years later, when he was aged 62, that John Alcock undertook to do the same thing again. He was suffering from bronchial trouble and his medical advisor went to the length of forbidding him to walk but, with dogged determination, he arrived at Waters Green at 20 minutes past 10 o'clock on the Easter Monday. Five minutes later, he set off and he went backwards to Buxton again. This time it took three hours and 14 minutes and his arrival in Buxton was considerably hampered by the enormous crowd who got in his way. Hundreds had also lined the route from Macclesfield to the Spa Town. He was entertained to a champagne reception.

'Orrible Abduction

In the Autumn of 1825 Miss Frances Davies, the daughter of the headmaster of Macclesfield Grammar School, spent a holiday in Paris accompanied by her maternal uncle Mr Thomas Critchley, who was a Macclesfield silk mill owner and a banker.

In Paris, she made the acquaintance of Edward Wakefield, a man of good education and charming personality, who was a widower with four sons - one of whom held a position in the British Embassy there.

This charmer was a man of about 50, tall, of a commanding aspect and although Frances or "Fanny" as she was known was very much his junior, she soon yielded to him. He introduced her to the Parisian nightlife and, when he began to talk of love, she listened with approval and delight. In a very short time, she cast discretion to the winds and married him at a ceremony held at the British Embassy in Paris - without telling her family.

After a brief honeymoon, she returned to Macclesfield and her husband went to London where he had a residence. It was some weeks before the bride plucked up enough courage to tell her father. When she did, Wakefield was invited to Macclesfield and, after initial problems, they settled in the town.

The following year, one of his sons, Edward Gibbon Wakefield, visited his father and new mother in Macclesfield. He had relinquished his secretaryship at the Embassy and was ambitious for a Parliamentary career.

He was eloquent and ambitious, daring and unscrupulous.

Young Gibbon knew that the Parliamentary Reform Bill would give Macclesfield two Members of Parliament and he wanted to enlist the influence of the town's headmaster. The chief obstacle in his was lack of funds.

Macclesfield's mills were having a lean time of it because of the tariff duties, so the hopeful candidate got some practice for a hoped-for parliamentary career by making a speech to Macclesfield millworkers, denouncing the tariffs. That same night, after his speech, he told his stepmother (who was about his own age) that he intended to stand as Member of Parliament for Macclesfield. Wakefield told her he was short of funds and, jokingly, said he needed to marry a rich heiress like the one he had seen driving in her carriage along Chestergate the day before. She was Miss Ellen Turner of Shrigley Hall, a young lady who had only days before reached the age of 16.

Just who decided what on that fateful evening is far from certain, but later on , Wakefield was to admit that from that evening he set about making plans to carry off Ellen.

He enlisted the help of his stepmother and also one of his brothers, William, and his valet - a Frenchman called Thevenot. They learned that the heiress went to school in Liverpool so, after laying their plans, went to Warrington and at the Nag's Head, Sankey Street, dressed the valet in the livery of a coachman from Shrigley Hall. They hired a coach and sent him to Ellen's school at Liverpool with a message purporting to be from the family attorney.

This said that her mother was paralysed and wished to see her daughter urgently. So she went with the Frenchman to the Albion Hotel, Manchester, on the evening of March 7th, 1826.

Ellen sat alone at the hotel, eating a meal, when Wakefield introduced himself and said he came from her father (who was the High Sheriff of Cheshire) who had asked him to tell her he was a ruined man. Two banks he was involved with were bankrupt and Shrigley Hall had to be sold. Her father (said Wakefield) was hiding in Yorkshire from the bailiffs.

Wakefield told her there was a way to save her father and produced many forged documents which showed Wakefield had a rich uncle in Kendal who was willing to advance £60,000 to her father.

The only condition was that she should become Wakefield's wife.

Ellen agreed and allowed him to take her to Gretna Green where a marriage ceremony was held by a blacksmith called David Laing. They began their journey home but Wakefield did not take her to Shrigley Hall but to London, then Calais, where they took apartments at Quillac's Hotel.

On March 8th, Mr Turner received a letter from the headmistress at Liverpool saying how sorry she was about the illness. Not surprisingly, this caused considerable alarm and Mr Turner, Thomas Critchley and two servants set off for Liverpool where the headmistress described the events.

Police were informed and, after a number of weeks, the couple were traced to Calais. Ellen was told of the deception and was heartbroken. Wakefield professed he had not touched the girl, but was arrested and brought to Lancaster Gaol to await trial on a charge of abduction. The young Miss Turner went back to Shrigley Park.

The trial of Wakefield caused a nationwide sensation and several of the most brilliant and distinguished men in the legal world took part.

Wakefield was sentenced to three years' prison at Newgate and his brother, William, received a similar sentence to be passed at Lancaster. Owing to the fact that Mrs Wakefield had taken no active part in the carrying off of Miss Turner, she was pronounced guilty but never brought before the judge for sentence - tantamount to an acquittal.

A special Act of Parliament was afterwards passed, annulling the Gretna Green marriage.

Two years later, Miss Turner was happily married, and the rest of her life was passed in happiness. The couple lived at a house on the Macclesfield to Leek Road at Fools Nook.

Headmaster Davies never recovered and became mentally ill - never to resume his duties at Macclesfield Grammar School.

Six months after the trial, Wakefield's family were allowed to see him at Newgate and noticed a terrible change in his appearance. The sights he witnessed in Newgate, and the experiences he gained, were used later in his efforts to improve the condition of British gaols.

After his release, he published a book "Punishment of Death in the Metropolis" in which he described the nurseries of crime and schools for thieves in London (Whitehall, St Giles and parts of Westminster). He wrote this in 1831 and it is believed Charles Dickens (who published Oliver Twist in 1838) was inspired by it to create the characters of Fagin, Nancy, Sykes, and the rest.

On his release, Wakefield went to North America where he was appointed assistant to the Governor General and he became a Canadian Member of Parliament in 1843 - without the help of a rich heiress.

The Canadian Collossus

Just before the turn of the century, a fat man came to Macclesfield.

His name was Leo Whitton and he was a professional freak. Weighing 52 stones he was advertised as the fattest man in the world and went by the name of the Canadian Collossus.

Leo was born in Canada and became a butcher by trade. He married and had six children but his weight got the better of him and he could no longer carry on his trade because he simply could not move about ! He began exhibiting himself in fairground sideshows and circuses and, after a while, he came to England where there were more towns within a closer proximity.

Leo Witton pictured in the rear yard of the Orange
Tree Inn, Macclesfield.

When he arrived by train from Manchester he caused quite a stir. It was with much difficulty he was eventually squeezed out of the carriage door and he was placed upon a coal cart hired from the nearby sidings.

He went to stay in lodgings at the Orange Tree Inn, Mill Lane, and there he remained for three years before he died of heart attack at the age of 43.

Just why he chose to stay in Macclesfield is not recorded, but he did charge people to come in to see him, and leaflets were freely distributed around the town.

He was friendly with another fairground freak, a midget who went by the name of Tiny Tim and they were known as the biggest and the smallest in the land. Tim also stayed at Macclesfield and when he died some years after Leo, was buried alongside him in a grave which can still be seen at Macclesfield Cemetery.

When Leo died, a window and part of the wall had to be taken out of the side of the public house and a block and tackle was used to lift the huge coffin, manufactured specially by the undertaker, Mr Lowe, of Sunderland Street. The coffin was placed on a brewer's cart and the block and tackle was also used to lower the coffin into the grave.

The funeral of Leo Witton at Macclesfield Cemetery. Note the size of the coffin and the block and tackle used to lower the coffin into the ground.

Next page

Inside Josiah Smale's silk mill in George Street. Nearest the camera is Mrs Mary Bradbury and behind her is Mrs Rachel Bradbury. Also, weaver George Newton, apprentice Norman Reece, tackler William Nadin.

9 Customs and Traditions

Heaving

On Monday and Tuesday in Easter week, the old custom of "Heaving" was carried out in and around Macclesfield, and this strange custom has a direct link with Queen Eleanor. A party of men presented themselves on the first day at each house in the town with a chair and forced every female to be seated. Then they were lifted three times amid cheering. The reward of a kiss or a fine of a few pennies was imposed and then a written statement barring a repetition of the ceremony was given. The next day it was the ladies' turn to do the same but they also guarded every entrance to the town and everyone walking or riding had to submit to them. This was designed to represent Jesus' resurrection and originally the lifters used to join hands across each other's wrists to form a 'throne'. Only later was a chair used. The tradition carried on until the 1800's.

But what of Queen Eleanor? In the year 1275, she consented to seven of her ladies of honour and other of her attendants lifting Edward while he was in bed on Easter Monday. They extracted from him gift of 14 shillings - a princely sum.

When Eleanor became Lady of the Manor of Macclesfield, her followers took it upon themselves to preserve this ritual in her honour.

Treacle Town

During the early 19th century there was, again, much distress in Macclesfield and it is during this period that Macclesfield was given the nickname of "Treacle Town"

The popular theory of how Macclesfield came to be called "Treacle Town" has always been, quite simply, that a barrel of treacle fell off a cart in Mill Street and its contents spilled. The townsfolk rushed to lick it up. This is correct as far as it goes but this brief story does not reflect the background of hardship, deprivation and hunger that prevailed in the town in the 1820s.

I have tried to find some documented evidence of this for many years, but I could come across only folklore and fantasy and no facts - until quite recently when I happened to unearth an article written by John Ray, an historian, for the *London Journal* of 1830. He told of the origins of "Treacle Town" and of "Bear Town" for near-neighbour Congleton.

Macclesfield people, when coming across someone from Congleton, would shout out the rhyme,"Congleton rare, Congleton rare, sold the Church Bible to buy a new bear". In retaliation the Congletonians would reply,"Treacle - has our bell rung?" accompanying the query with a pantomimic action suggesting and imitating the sucking of treacle from the forefinger of the right hand.

The cause of these two appellations "Bear Town" and Treacle Town are thus, relates our historian: not during all periods of its history did Macclesfield have the reputation of being such a poverty-stricken borough as in the 1820s, when hard times came to the town. Owing to the great reduction in the duties on thrown silk and manufactured silks imported from foreign countries, the trade of Macclesfield rapidly declined and the town quickly sank to a terribly depressed condition. The people were compelled to endure great poverty, deprivation and hunger. The condition of the silk workers was so bad that bread and treacle was their staple diet, and very many could not get even that humble fare.

There is a tradition that during those dark days in the history of the town, a large cask of molasses became overturned near to a grocer's shop in Mill Street and the sweet and succulent syrup emptied itself into the gutter. Seizing the opportunity, the famished Silkites greedily devoured the treacle - some bringing slices of bread which they dipped in the juicy stuff, and others using their fingers, which they dipped in the luscious liquid, ever and anon anxiously asking each other, "Has our bell rung?" referring to the factory bell which summoned them to their daily labours. In those days children went to the mill at a very early age and had to commence work at six o'clock in the morning. It was quite a usual thing for the youngsters to sally forth in the early hours of the day with a slice of bread and treacle (a treacle buck or a treacle butty) which they would devour on their way to the factory.

This story is backed up in no small way by a book which describes the life, of all people, a Lancashire cotton worker! In "A Memoir of Robert Blincoe" first published in 1832, the story is told of the cotton worker (who, incidentally, died at the home of his daughter in Gunco Lane, Macclesfield) and mentions the tradition of mills supplying barrels of treacle for workers to dip their own bread into.

And as for Beartown? The people of Congleton were passionately fond of bear-baiting and, as the rhyme says, sold the Church bible to buy a bear.

Fairs

Fairs and markets were intermingled. At the fairs there was much buying and selling, and Macclesfield has been fortunate in having both fairs and markets for over 800 years.

Most famous of all Macclesfield's fairs is, of course, Barnaby. Over the past 200 years it was the main holiday for the mill workers but has been a time for celebration for centuries. Indeed, what inhabitant of Macclesfield is there, even now, who is not familiar with the name Barnaby?

A fine picture of the Wakes Fair in the Waters.
Note the sideshows on the left. The photograph
was taken from the approach to the Central
Station.

But why is it called Barnaby?

Saints' Days have had their ups and downs in Christian history. Saint Barnabus is commemorated on June 11, but Barnaby is now the Monday to the Longest Day, June 21st. When roads were few and far between and travel was difficult, holy days gave opportunity not only for worship but also for business and pleasure. Hence cattle fairs at particular times and places.

Of the nine fairs that were held in Macclesfield (most are now defunct) Barnaby is one of the two oldest and, it will be observed , the present Barnaby holiday does not fall on June 11 but 11 days later. The reason for this is that the natural year of recurring seasons does not consist of an exact number of days and, as the old calendar did not make proper allowance for this,it gradually got more and more out of step. This was corrected in 1752, by which time Barnabus Day, June 11th, was falling at midsummer. In that year, the eleven days between September 2nd and 14th were omitted and so, in the following year, St Barnabus Day was eleven days before mid summer. The local holiday was still fixed at midsummer and the old name, Barnaby, though now a misnomer, was still applied. And so it is to this day.

Barnaby Fair and the May Fair were held in the Waters (the area named because of the river that flowed through, now under, it).

Mr John Earles described a Barnaby Fair in early Victorian times thus: "The entrance to the fairground in Sunderland Street was lined on both sides by the vendors of nuts and gingerbread, and stalls, gaily lit up and laden with toys, formed an attractive introduction to the delights to be enjoyed in the Waters. Imagine yourself in a densely packed, heterogeneous mass of humanity which completely fills the fairgrounds and extends to the top of the Wallgate and to Hibel Road, and which swings you to and fro, and in and out, and any way but the right one. Conjure up in your mind an inferno of hideous noises, the firing of guns and the ringing of bells, the squeaking of toy trumpets and the conflicting music of half a dozen bands and you will have a fair idea of Barnaby Fair in the olden times. Here is what you might see:

A gaily-illuminated booth is a travelling menagerie or wild beast show on the front of which a red-faced and brazen-voiced man invites you to enter and view the wild and untamed African lion, which bit off a keeper's head a month ago. To add to the colour the lion is depicted in lurid colours, on the front of the show, being burned with red hot irons to induce him to drop his victim.

Here may be a giantess, a living skeleton, and a dwarf two feet high, which may each be viewed for the small charge of one penny.

That immense wooden booth is Richardson's Theatre, or perhaps Snape's Temple of Tragedy, in which, for the outlay of a few coppers, you may see melodrama, with three murders and a ghost, a pantomime and several comic songs, all performed in an hour by "London actors of great eminence".

The crowd of people, all bent on enjoying themselves in their own fashion, is made up of persons of every rank and grade in society. The respectable silk weaver, with his wife and children, who have been saving up their pence for weeks in anticipation of the joys of the fair, may be seen pushing and crushing to get into the show, where Holden's Mechanical Performing Marionettes are being exhibited. Here is a band of well dressed young bucks of the town bent on mischief, and there you may see stalwart and ruddy young farmers from Gawsworth and Wildboarclough who, having sold their cattle and horses in the morning, and partaken freely of the liquor at the Cross Keys, Nag's Head or Roundhouse in the afternoon, are crowding to the swingboats, hobby horses or shooting galleries, closely followed by several furtive and nimble-fingered pickpockets who are only waiting for a suitable opportunity to abstract the money from their pockets. And here, also, are to be found gaily dressed, painted and powdered women, who are also keenly on the lookout for some foolish or half-fuddled young countryman, round whom they may spread their net of enchantment prior to fleecing him of his honour and purse, and too often alas, of his health and future happiness in addition.

Mr Earles bemoans the fact that in his time (the early 20th century) much of Macclesfield Fair's ancient glory had departed. Today it is but a pathetic number of modern amusements huddled together in the railway station car park. It has all but died.

Carnival Parade

Macclesfield's Carnivals of yesteryear attracted thousands upon thousands of spectators from all over Cheshire, Staffordshire and South Manchester.

They re-started in 1925, the principal aim being to raise funds for Macclesfield Infirmary. The procession of floats, jazz bands, fancy dress characters, the Silk Queen for the year and eight Silk Princesses (chosen from various silk mills in the town) began, fittingly, from the Infirmary. The finish was at South Park, where the fun continued throughout the day and culminated in an evening firework display.

The procession used to wend its way up Cumberland Street into Prestbury Road, down Chestergate to the Market Place, Jordangate and Hibel Road, then along Commercial Road into the Waters. The rest of the route was through Sunderland Street, Park Green,

The Silk Queen and retinue, 1930s

The Beach Brigade Prize Jazz Band in Waterloo Street.

Frosts Prize Jazz Band and the Silk Town Prize Jazz Band.

A tableau entitled "Sunset on the Nile".

The year is 1932 and the Silk Queen, Miss Brenda Goodwin, her retinue and the Princesses line up at the Infirmary steps ready for the big parade around Macclesfield.

The Heatherbells Jazz Band

The "Marcovitch Cigarette Girls" and other participants.

The entire Silk Queen ensemble on the Infirmary Steps.

Pride of place in every Macclesfield Carnival went to these two popular characters - the Hazel Grove Twins. They raised £100s for the Infirmary over the years and, while the Carnival had the Silk Queen and the Silk Princesses, the loudest cheer always went to these two. If you could not make them laugh you had to pay a forfeit.

A Macclesfield Silk Queen of the 1930s, Iris Barnes.

Annie Wardle, the "Spirit of the Carnival" pictured in Cumberland Street.

Mill Lane, Cross Street, Coronation Street, High Street, down Old Park Lane, Mill Street, Chestergate, Catherine Street, Bond Street, and into South Park.

The average length was about two miles from fronto to tail.

In the weeks after the event, the Silk Queen, her retinue and some of the officials would tour surrounding villages by North Western bus, specially decorated for the occasion.

J. Sigley and Sons, Cardboard Box manufacturers of Pickford Street and Compton Box Mill, asked the crowds to buy Macclesfield Silk and support local industries. Mr Joe Sigley is third from the right.

One of the floats - the "Electric Vehicle" - supplied by the Electricity Company of Macclesfield.

Macclesfield Football Club

For many years, Macclesfield Football Club had a field at Bowfield Lane, now Victoria Road. Originally, they had been the Macclesfield Volunteers Football Team, who played under Rugby rules, but afterwards adopted the Association code and ultimately became absorbed into Macclesfield Football Club.

At one time, the member of Parliament, Colonel Bromley Davenport, D.S.O, played in the team.

The club moved to its present site, The Moss Rose, in 1891.

Fashions change... and so do football supporters. This picture was taken in the very early years of the twentieth century shows ladies in their Sunday best watching Macclesfield Town Football Club.

1924-25:back: W.Fitchett, Dalton (res),referee, linesman, C. Burgess, H. Wood, Vigrass, C.B. Twemlow, Barnett (res). Front: F. Wood, J. Morris, V. Fowenther, H. Kelly, E. Collison (capt.), S. Mellor, A. Forrest.

Scene from the Cheshire Senior Cup Final on April 12th, 1930, when Macclesfield beat Nantwich at Crewe. Stanton and Taylor (Macc), Thompson and Sewell (Nantwich) and Johnston (Macc). Note the spectators on the stand roof.

After winning the Cheshire Senior Cup against Northwich, 1940. Players, back row: R. Hackney, G. Daniels, C. Pitt, Hamlett, Rosson, Crawshaw, Harrop. Front: C. James, T. Beswick. E. Davies (capt), E.A. Cock, C. Barton (trainer).

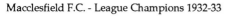

Macclesfield F.C. - League Champions 1932-33

10 Street Names

What's in a Name?

From the Domesday Book onwards, the history of Macclesfield is well chronicled but it is that dark period before the Conqueror which is more of a mystery. If the tiny village on the escarpment was once called Hameston (and local tradition is always a good pointer to fact for the historian) then why did it change its name to Macclesfield? The name has had various spellings over the years and some of these can be explained by the writers putting down a phonetic version of the name. But it could also give us a clue to its origins.

There are early records of the town's name being variously spelt as Makeselfeld (Royal Charter dated at Rothelan, 16th December 1283); as Makelisfield (Harl. MS mmlxxii); the Dieulacrese Chronicles say that in 1268 A.D Hugh Carpenter made a gift to the Abbey of Dieulacrese (north of Leek) an acre of land in Maxfield bought of Richard Carter; and an Elizabethan poet, Richard Robinson, in his "Golden Mirrur" refers to the town as "Marfield".

So why "Macclesfield"? There are a number of theories, and theories they must be for there is nothing recorded to make them facts. One idea is that it derived from Magna Ecclesia Field, being an extension of the mother church at Prestbury (or Priest's Burgh) while Dr C. Stella Davies states that Macca is a personal name and the head man of the local tribe may have been named "Macca".

My own theory is not so straightforward, I'm afraid. It stems from Macclesfield's position within the kingdom of Mercia. Around 550 A.D our little village on the hill was brought in to the Ancient Kingdom of Mercia by force. Warriors from the tribe known as the Angles advanced to take the village and the area became an outpost of the Mercian kingdom. The Mercia boundary was known as the Mark and these people became known as the men of the Markenric or Mearkenland.

Another word for boundary is "Lyme" and Lyme Green, just south of Macclesfield, lends extra support to the boundary theory: I believe "Macclesfield" was originally the Mercian's Mark in the Field.

Other spellings of this word "Mark" have been found as "marc" and "Mak" and the field would have been a clearing. The original meaning of the word "Mark" was a stone, used as a boundary "mark" and so we have the Mercian boundary stone in the clearing - at the most northerly tip of that ancient kingdom. The Nineteenth century writer Heywood

Stanley Street (formerly Dog Lane) during demolition to make way for the Grosvenor Centre.

Peel Street, Macclesfield, looking to Park Lane. The Peels Arms is on the left and a milkman can be seen delivering milk in churns on the back of his cart, pulled by a donkey.

Mill Street looking towards Stanley Street (top right). Padlock Brown's ironmongers is recognisable by the large padlock sign and this was where the MacDonald's Restaurant now is. Opposite Padlock Brown's, Castle Street was developed in the early 1920s but on this photograph was not even a glimmer in the Town Clerk's eyes.

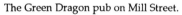

The Green Dragon pub on Mill Street.

A scene over the Commercial Road area, before these terraced homes were demolished to make way for the Victoria Park development.

Most of the shops to the left of the new Town Hall have now been demolished. From the Market Place, the way in to the Shambles and Gutters was through either the Union or Unicorn Gateways. The Unicorn Gateway, named after the Unicorn Inn, can just be seen to the left of the lighter coloured building. This photograph, taken about 1903 was from the corner of Chestergate.

Stanley Street, Macclesfield, in 1934 Bill Bayley, Charlie Watson and Jack Sutton stand outside Watson's Butchers shop. Prime pork was 10d a lb and chilled beef could be bought from between 4d and 10d a lb.

Inside the Co-Op stores in Sunderland Street, about 1905.

Summer says "Marked boundary place names frequently denote the limits of primitive settlements, e.g. Mark Oak. There is an instance of a forest court held in a clearing by a marc tree."

Names changed by Time

We have mentioned some names already that Time has changed, for better and worse. Names like The Shambles and The Gutters and Godyaff Lane are all now lost, and there are many casualties:

Worth Hall: In the middle of Chestergate, on the site of the Derby Arms, now owned by Kennings, was an old mansion owned by the Savage family, which is said to have been the residence of Thomas Savage, Archbishop of York.

Cockshute Lane: is now Hibel Road and was once a narrow, dark and steep lane leading from Jordangate to Hurdsfield and to the Kings Mill in the Waters. Its name probably derives from the fowl that were taken from town to the river, via this lane, or from the pactice of cock-fighting around here.

Back Street: now King Edward Street, which once contained many fine houses owned by the gentry.

Dog Lane: was later, in 1826 called Stanley Street on account of the Stanleys of Alderley, and was demolished in the late 1960's to make way for the Grosvenor Centre. It was called Dog Lane because the kennels for the Macclesfield Castle were here - these held the hunting dogs for the Master. It was, later, a street that contained many taverns and lodging houses.

Barn Street: Later Derby Street (after the Earl of Derby) and now Churchill Way. The name Barn Street is obvious. Whether the barn was the one where Macclesfield people had to buy their corn is a matter for debate.

Cockatrice Hall: in Mill Street, opposite the Bears Head. A large hall, named after a monster with a lizard's body and the head of a cockerel , about which very little is known. It was probably built about the same time as the Castle but there is little, if any, documentation.

Pudding Bag Street: the street is now called Lower Exchange Street, at the back of the Normid Superstore, which connects Mill Street with Boden Street. Thus named because it was a cul-de-sac, shaped like a pudding bag.

Spitalfields: the passage that connected Roe Street with Newgate (now the loading area for Sainsbury's). It was later called Prospect Buildings. Named after the London Spitalfields, it was where the Macclesfield silk throwers congregated.

St Anne's Well: once a well in Park Lane for the inhabitants of the area, near Higginbotham Street. Macclesfield had many wells at one time. Churchwallgate was formerly Church Well gate and supplied inhabitants around the old Castle. The Castle Inn used to be referred to as the "Well's Mouth".

Hallefield: where the old baths and washhouse is situated, probably once called Hulley's Field - Hulley being a common Macclesfield name (e.g. Hulley Road).

Clock Alley: a narrow street between Commercial Road and Thorp's mill where a large clock was placed so that workpeople would have no excuse for being late!

The Old Workhouse: Where Arighi Bianchi's premises now stand. Later, the workhouse went to Prestbury Road and later became West Park hospital.

The Town Field: where West Park now is and where horse races used to be held.

Gallows Field: the district around Chester Road from St Alban's R.C.Church up to Broken Cross was known thus and tradition has it that executions took place here.

Chestergate, looking from the Market. Parr's Bank is on the left and Pott and Thomson's famous coffee shop is on the right.

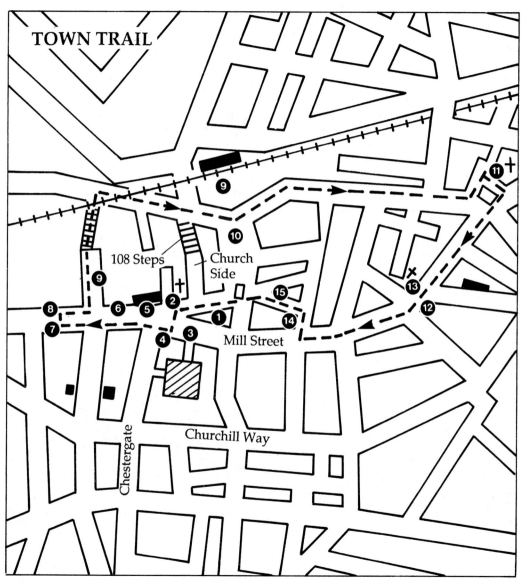

TOWN TRAIL

108 Steps
Church Side

9

Chestergate

Mill Street

Churchill Way

1. Start in front of the Parish Church, by the Market Cross. The church was founded by Queen Eleanor.

2. The gravestones in front of the Church are of interest and can be walked around.

3. The Market Place (in front of the Town Hall) was once a thriving commercial sector where all kinds of merchandise was sold. The entrance to the Grosvenor Centre is where Stanley Street used to be (once called Dog Lane because of the Castle kennels for the hunting dogs).

4. The modern Natwest building was once Parr's Bank and, just around the corner in Chestergate, was the ancient Sun Inn.

5. The Town Hall, built in 1824, is on the site of the Guildhall.

6. Just to its side used to be the Unicorn Gateway leading to the Gutters, where people traded for hundreds of years. Here, the Plague was rife.

7. Across the road, past the Macclesfield Arms (where a young Queen Victoria once stayed) is Cumberland House where the Duke of Cumberland bedded down while in pursuit of Bonnie Prince Charlie.

8. Jordangate House (1728).

9. Go down picturesque Brunswick Hill (be careful if it's icy though!) into the Waters and Sunderland Street. Central Station (once the Cross Keys Hotel site) was rebuilt in the 1960s.

10. Fairs have been held in Waters Green since before Elizabethan days.

11. Along Sunderland Street to Park Green. The Gradus building was formerly Frost's Mill.

12. Towards Mill Street. Opposite the United Reform Church, in front of the Library, was an ornate cast iron fountain.

13. Silk House, a modern building where Charles Roe's Depot Mill stood, is by the side of the church.

14. Up Mill Street, Palace Yard (past Mothercare) was the entrance to Macclesfield Castle.

15. Down steep Backwallgate (some of the Castle stone can be seen in the wall) to the Castle Inn, where the Castle's ancient keys are.

Please note: Macclesfield is not a flat town - there are some steep hills to negotiate and a number of steps. The Market Place, Mill Street and Sunderland Street sections into Waters Green could be negotiated in a wheelchair but not the Brunswick Hill section.

MACCLESFIELD
old and new

The Town Hall, late 1920s. The now demolished
Angel Hotel is seen far left.

The Town Hall just prior to the
modern extension for offices.

The fountain in front of the Chadwick Free Library
was pulled down during the second world war
and mettled down for the war effort, although
none of it was ever used. Two small ornamental
birds were saved.

Park Green with, on the right, Dr Somerville's residence - later the registry office. St Paul's church is in the background.

Looking up to Park Lane. Note the two carters who have stopped to have a chat and the three girls on the right under the sign that reads "Parkers Dental Surgery". To the left is Dr Somerville's residence.

11 Prestbury and District

There was undoubtedly a settlement at Prestbury (the Saxon name meaning Priest's Town) before the Norman Conquest.

However, there is no mention of this Priest's Town in the Domesday Survey and this gives rise to the conjecture that it was one of many towns and villages that was laid to waste by the conquering forces.

In the 12th century the manor of Prestbury seems to have been included with the church when the latter was given to the Abbey of St Werburgh at Chester and it remained under the ownership of the Abbey until the dissolution of the monasteries in 1537.

At some time in the 15th century, if not earlier, the Prestbury lands were leased to the Leghs of Adlington who farmed the area and after the reformation Prestbury came under the control of the newly created Dean and Chapter of Chester. In 1553 they were made over to Sir Richard Cotton and his family and two years later he granted them to Richard Grosvenor Esq and John Grosvenor, his brother, for an annual rent of £100.

In 1579 Queen Elizabeth declared that the grant to Sir Richard Cotton had been illegal and so the lands were granted to Sir George Caveley, George Cotton, Hugh Cholmondely, Thomas Legh, Henry Mainwaring, John Nuthall and Richard Hurleston and their heirs for annual rental.

These were people known as fee-farmers who, after several years of working the land, decided to give it all over to Thomas Legh and his heirs (apart from some land in Chelford and Astle). Much of this land has remained in the possession of the Legh family through to the present day.

In 1880, the village of Prestbury was described as consisting of "one long street, at one end of which is Butley Hall ... and at the other end Prestbury Hall. The latter was for many years the home of Dr James Hope, well known physician, who was born at Stockport in 1801 where his father, Mr Thomas Hope, was in business as a merchant and manufacturer. Dr Hope was partly educated at Macclesfield Grammar School under Dr Davies. The Hall is now the residence of Richardson Adrew, Esq."

Now, of course, the village has grown considerably but it still retains much of its old charm. It has been said of Prestbury that there are more good shops and restaurants in its main street than anywhere else in Britain.

Here we see some pictures of Prestbury of old and also some shots that give an idea of what the countryside around Macclesfield used to be like in those halcyon days long ago.

The two-story "magpie" design house opposite the church is now a bank.

The Temperance Hotel, Prestbury - now the White House Restaurant.

The ladies stroll along the tree-lined road outside the Admiral Rodney.

Even in the 1890s, Prestbury could boast "Ye Olde Shoppes".

Lovely Gawsworth village, so full of romance. This picture was taken before 1900.

Walker Barn in the hills above Macclesfield. The pub is the Setter Dog, pictured in the 1930s.

Many Macclesfield people would walk to Dane Bridge before the internal combustion engine made the going easier. In this picture taken about 1903 a young Maxonian called George Genders pauses by the bridge.

12 Bollington

The Happy Valley

The township of Bollington nestles at the foot of the Kerridge Hills, with the famous White Nancy landmark perched proudly on top.

There's nothing in the Domesday Survey about Bollington but it is thought to date back to Saxon times. Certainly there have been a number of discoveries of early man in and around the area.

High Street

Palmerston Street in the 1940s

Bollington came under the religious domination of Prestbury until 1842 when Queen Victoria made the parish of St. John.

Unlike big sister Macclesfield, just down the road, Bollington owes its industrial prosperity to cotton, not silk. Cotton spinning had been the major trade until the last cotton mill closed in 1960.

But it is the "folly" known as White Nancy which draws so much interest in the area. Built by the Gaskell family on a site undoubtedly used by our ancestors for beacons and probably pagan ceremonies, the white "sugarloaf" structure is thought to have been built to commemorate Waterloo. Its name derives from either a member of the Gaskell family or from "White Ordnance".

A young lady strolls by Ingersley Vale in about the year 1919.

An ivy covered canal bridge over Grimshaw Lane. 91

School Brow, Bollington

The canal at Beeston Mount. Notice the farmer haymaking with his two horses.

The aqueduct

On Kerridge by White Nancy in the 1930s

Children in Adlington Road, 1895.